HONOURING THY *self*

TANYA TURTON

Copyright © 2020 Tanya Turton

Copyright remains the property of the author
and apart from any fair dealing for the purposes
of private study, research, criticism or review, as
permitted under the Copyright Act, no part may be
reproduced by any process without written permission.
All inquiries should be made to the author.

Typeset & Cover by Chain of Hearts Creative

National Library of Australia - ISBN-978-0-6452064-0-1

HONOURING THY SELF

In the thought of self to be of more importance than anyone or any-thing to be seeing of, would this not be received as your knowing that you are the only one that is to be encouraged from within, to speak these words to express as,

I AM the worthiest to feel, know & see.

OUR SPOKEN TRUTH

It is to offer here that one is to feel this resistance in reaction to these words to speak regarding thy self to be the utmost shall we say in their eyes to BEHOLD. It is in this internal reaction to hear of the self being spoken of in such a grand way, as to think of self to be better than most it appears to us to be witnessing into that you would choose these words to mean.

Know of this dear one, interpret these words never as wrong, for it is that they are not.

In our offering to be seen as an acceptance from you, it is often in this earthly presence that holds you, that you feel yourself responding unwillingly at times, yet almost as if to be on auto pilot to react... your visual cues and this thinking mind who is always surveying, judging and even critising all opportunities and suggestions presented to you, and it appears to us that both have held you captive like a hostage in this space to overrule your truths and grand love that you be. And it is usually this physical structure that doubts and fears, who is stubborn or resistant to change that is intercepting this holy voice, the voice of love that speaks to be heard in truth. In this space of true connection, you will find the spiritual heart, the forgiving heart, the real god's love space, the speaker's space that is to be yours to know of within. Feel this sequence of events unfold through the opening and awareness of this path to all aspects of your heart, revealing to you this desire to begin honouring thy self as this sovereign being of love and light that you BE. In this your loving voice is where you shall begin, you should turn to listen intently to all words that are uttered in this quietness of yours to be heard.

More to offer......

OUR SPOKEN TRUTH;

Feel this loving space {YOUR HEART SPACE}, as uniquely yours to be of absolute love, reminding you to feel this strong desire of unison between us, and who it is you truly are once more. Be this vibration to always emit love, to speak this love as yours eternally known. Let yourself be guided inwardly, to know it as yours, and only yours to experience.

It is in this grand dwelling of connection, that you will negate all personal insults, your own included and those from others that have offered you suggestions or meanings to evoke out of you an experience to hear, see, even to re-live this that is not truly you.

Dwell no more into beliefs that no longer serve you as your own to know.

For it is NOW your time to stand fully and truthfully into belief's of your own, and to enter this temple that sits majestically, with the doors wide open within your loving heart to see.

We see you there to sit upon this throne, {unsure we witness at times, asking if you are worthy to call of it as your own}.

Know dear one it is yours to always see this place to rest, to speak, to evolve and grow.

It is here that one must listen to the whispers of this soul, honouring this human that has courageously revealed this being of love & light.

To allow herself/ himself once again; to speak out loud these righteous words of love to thy self.

I HONOUR THEE.
I AM.

These words we present to you as a true representation of self to hear; **'you are the King/Queen within. You are the most if not always the more that you see. You are the receiver of everything that is you and one should be willing and allowing of self to be the speaker in the boldest, grandest way that she/he can find to be heard from this voice of yours to offer'.**

Let yourself know in all this glory that you be, that it is of only you that we see standing into her/or his perfection of this alluring knowing to us to be. We see you as truly magnificent and in the honouring of thy self to be a validation within you to know of this you must **'we will see you to ever shine always in the brightest way possible'.**

CHAPTER ONE

HELLO! WHO ARE YOU? GETTING TO KNOW ME.

You offer here in this space to receive that I AM the one that I must in all capabilities and possibilities be seeing of myself as always complete.

YES, let us offer this suggestion in other ways in which to say, to be steady within oneself to know, assured of herself, belief undeniable as to who and what it is that you are, I AM correct, balanced within, pronounced from within to see self as certain, love spoken, and enticed truly by oneself to see. Be encouraged here in this space of acknowledgement to feel, to receive your own words to speak in the way as to honour this that you are ever present within to see self as. Your words of voice and description are powerful shall we say, to be the ever-encompassing feeling to surround you in an acceptance from this form to speak in words of acknowledgement to be yours to accept.

If you have not ever or are not able to utter words in a profound way of which it would be to describe yourself as this honoured creature to be. Let us speak to offer this suggestion {resistance may be present within the many that have been held into a captive way to think as to always put others before themselves or that others are the ones that are more worthy}. Leaders, family or friends, religious beliefs into gods, goddesses or buddas and teachers of ancient wisdoms, old residues that show up in your psyche from past lifetimes lived into as remembrances stored in cellular receiving's are all to impact many thinking minds. And it is in a relinquishing of this self to be lesser or not of equal consideration to these so thought to be offered often to you as to be your devoted, loved or chosen hierarchy / leaders / gods / influencers as such.

It is and never was intended to be seen to be bowing down to or shall we say in another way to be ever receiving to these in only to be thought of as less than any other. In our truth offered to speak into, you are a blessed being of this honourable self that speaks, and the all that many appear to relay to self to be of a higher deity or entity to be over you, this you shall know they are not, nor never will be grander than thee.

It is not in this way to appear to speak of these offerings as such to disrespect the information that the many of you have deliberately received. As in either an asking or spoken to grow into a following from within, to be a participate into this way in which to think of themselves to be in need of these Powerheads, Ancestors, Gods, Christ or the all mighty to be thought of as the seers that you are needing to live your loves/and lives through their visions of self to be.

For is it not often repeated to hear, that they are to be the eyes that see only the best within another to be presented.

You are often told that you are the creation of this righteous god.

Are you not?

We wish not to disrespect you; in this we speak regarding your opinion, beliefs, or long-standing involvement as to the religious aspect or family traditions of self to be thinking into. If one can adjust their acceptance in this that one sees, to realise this, they themselves are their gods within that speak.

You are the almighty within. You are to honour this King or Queen shall we say to use these titles to speak, for they are to be the rulers that you are to honour within.

Bow down or be felt belittled not ever to another to feel as if to believe of them to be a worthiness in more or power to speak as them to be. For it is spoken, they are to be ever present in this that you are to respect to see as always, an entitlement to be, and in this way yours asked to be present for you to suggest as a willingness to be yours to determine as this in all to see.

> *You are not these words spoken of by another.*

Your words are hesitant it is we feel, to voice or even to think into or allow oneself to even begin to comprehend a thought as such, often these offerings to oneself have been handed down or passed down in many continuing generations of stories, traditions, and beliefs to be passed into. Let us say, that in a religious aspect we are not; for to wear an official title or name shall we say that it is unwilling to be this as us to see as a reference to. We are willing to be known as simply this to just be, for we are all wanting and willing in our becoming to be felt within you as this greater you that you be, but in many lifetimes, or occasions to speak on your behalf as to have been witness to be not in a space to feel like receiving this as a new way in which to think of self to be thought as, then....

Why now?

It is to be a constant stirring within many that we are to see, and you are being reminded into this that you are to be felt as more or in a simple way to express from within **'that there has to be more than this as I see it, does there not?'**

We hear the many of you to ask in this simple way, as to question your life or interactions upon this world with others, even in quiet contemplation of time spent within self as an asking of questions such as these to be heard that arise from within in just this suggestion from self to be released.

We are not to be the informers of one's thoughts to change; for of this we do not.

It is always to be told that in ones willingness to comprehend, to ask or to even notice a slight deterring away from the original way or old ways into which one was to think they will feel a touch of hesitation within to be in this position of which it feels to ask or question this that appears as an uncertainty or maybe a slight disbelief into of what it was that they thought they were.

Are we guided into this position to think this way?

If we were to say Yes to this in a certain knowing to be ours to offer this to think, that you are being persuaded by unthinking thoughts or thoughts that are not sincerely yours than we would suggest this to be not correct to think.

But in this to offer that YES, this intent is laying within you from your conception of self to become to this very moment of your time to rise to be seen or heard shall we offer then, that YES you are being guided but not in the way as to speak of by uncertainty or a power of persuasion or spells cast or misgivings in an unnatural way imposed upon one shall we say. This intent within you is the oblivious part of you, the spark of spirit that has remained undermined, unspoken or even truer as unheard by you in a willingness to hear to speak to even comprehend that you hold this decisiveness within……

An ethical way of which it is to be seen as yours in a complete honesty of, it is to be your internal ever-present guider of this eternal love that you are to you, to see & BE.

So, let us offer in these kind words here to add to this suggestion that YES you are ever guided; but never persuaded to be of a thought or suggestion that you are not willing to be or non-wanting of. For this stirring within you does not rise or become noticeable shall we say within the humanoid that you are until you so realise of this moment intentionally felt to be asked, seen, or felt from within this form that you hold yourself constructed into. So, YES, it is in your willingness to be feeling of this to be known or spoken of as your guidance system within, to be seen as your compass of directional understanding within this form that you are to be viewing of this self as you until in so time of it to be your now to want to realise, we offer to say that you shall.

To speak of this in this way feels like 'black magic' to speak.

IN this way in which one is to think, you shall.

WHY is this named as black magic, at times even a dishonesty or untrusting disbelief or mysterious evilness to be spoken of as?

In ones own way to think of black as to be an offering associated with darkness, death, evil, the unseeable or even unforbidden maybe it appears to one to think as this as an offering as hers or his own thoughts congested within self or simply encouraged by this of another to express. Does it not?

We are deliberate creators of self to become into this very essence of pure spirit source or self to be seeing. One is to have become from a certain understanding as to be from or of something it appears it is in your willingness to become that you did, this we know. So, is it fair to offer that all become out of a nothingness in which a certain darkness or sight to think into a nothingness to be presented in a dark or non-colour shall we say to be viewed upon? It is not us to be thought of in this way, for the darkness that all if everything that is to be thought of has contained within themselves to be a greater part of existence within this unique understanding of what it is that we are. One will always be in a position or willingness to evolve out into this light to be seen as a deliberate seeing against this backdrop of eternity that is to hold you complete in the seeing of this that you be to know of, that this is your formation of self shall we say into an existence that is held right within you. Eternally becoming the complete soul of which is to discover, to yearn, to crave, to expand into an understanding of self to be so large in existence within itself that it is unimaginable to the human eye or mind to comprehend this of oneself to be.

Of the magic part can we offer to you to comprehend this to ask, are you all not to be seen into this unseeing yet knowable ability to be magic within self to be allowing of this complete becoming into this that you so choose to be seen as magic. The divine within you is to be your heaven and blessed being, spirited parts of you to be ever resilient to the internal knowing of this that you think of yourself as not to be.

We see many of you sitting into this wonderment when first felt as you to hold of this creation of magic to be explained to us as a feeling to think into.

You are this holder of magical escape from certainty and a politeness of self to be thought of as human. For you are in the complete allowing of oneself {if and when willing} to enter this state of completeness. To be experienced as a space of non-thought, one that you must be willing or able to enter into, to feel this freedom into a trance like state or even as disbelief on your part that we hear many of you to offer here to us to describe of. This space is felt like no other to explain or offer description to.

It appears like magic from within that envelopes the outer casing giving away to a sense of nothingness to be felt as a form to hold self into. So, in this it is to hear, that yes it would be seen as a mystical experience by those of you that have a strong hold or grasp upon magic to be seen in an attempt to deceive or interpret as your thinking mind as a solidness to be the only way in which this human structure is to be. You are to be ever changing and continual in your evolving of this that you see yourself so righteous in your becoming of to be this human that you pretend to be the only part of which it is to see. So, let us offer here that in magic it is that we believe; to be used as a word to describe of us to be for we are sleight of hand, ever changing to reappear or disappear, we sense no limitations as to the space that appears present whether it is filled or not, we are the wand that one is to wave to realise of the magic that they possess shall we say as to refer to your thinking mind here to be just this, **for in the mind to think they shall.**

**What if I don't believe in magic to see?
It feels not real to me.**

WE offer magic to you to use as a word of mystical imaginary and belief into of what it is that one cannot see.

We are more to the inner seeing eye or heart to feel that see's shall we say. So, in one's beliefs to be not to see or to know, then they shall not. One is to be willing to picture themselves into a place of non-conformity that is guided by others and such a strong defiance within self to be thought of in no other way. You are the complete receiver of your many thoughts of this present self & life to be. So, be willing we say to receive many in what appears to be contradictions within this one's form to think of that it as to appear to be an indifference within this form to think of herself or himself to be.

You are very convincing in this way of which it is that you speak.

YES, it would appear to the unhearing ear to think of this to comment as this that we speak so confidently into. For let us offer that we are not seers of the many intrusions of thoughts in the human form to be offered to you in many moments of your accepting or rejecting throughout your physically observing day. We are deliberate creators of this that we chose to become and will and are to be. So, in this is a sturdiness in an unfathomable belief into this that we are formed from or more to be correct exact knowing of to exist of as to be seen into as this ONE that is to be the all that we are to be recognised within.

SO, to be so confidently placed as you would suggest within self it becomes a place of strength that is to rule you in a powerfulness of such undeniable force within you to know that you are unwavering to think of yourself as anything other than the one that is always in this place to be honouring of thy self to be seen as complete.

My conviction within self to speak this, feels unwilling.

One in this structured form who respects another's offerings or opinions over their own to be thought will always find themselves to be in this so-called position of unwillingness. It is allowed to spread through you in a sense of self not to be worthy or not in response to self to be wanting to hear, even in a place of steadiness from within to feel as if to even ask.

I am not important enough, or edgy enough, I feel not to fit in, not smart enough, or I do not think like they do……

Many offerings spoken this way to express a lack of self-worth to be, is often expressed by those of you that we are hearing of to speak about yourself in this way is to be the detrimental downgrading or denying of this form that you be, to be hesitant to think that you can. You are the responder to all thoughts that shall be offered or allowed to eventuate from within this body of presentation to offer to yourself to hear. It is to emerge, and it surely will this dependence upon this one that you be that you will wish to hear into not of another, but in only this 'I' that you are.

For you must not allow your dependency on another to speak or guide you to ever be a substitute for you, the real you in your voice of conviction shall we say here to express. Confidence grows and becomes of you, if you are to always welcome it into your thoughts of self to be allowing of it to become yourself to see yourself as encouraged by you.

In an unwillingness to view yourself in a different way to view, one will feel the depths of despair to say into thoughts of this that you are not enough, we are to offer here that your thoughts are your most powerful creation of transformation in this human to be.

In thoughts to think your heart must also be accepted as a true hearer to feel of this that you must think yourself be willing to hear.

> YOU ARE THE WORTHIEST BEING OF THIS LOVE, TO BE ENTITLED ALWAYS & EVER AS YOURS TO SEE YOURSELF IN.

To change ones veiw appears difficult, does it not?

In this statement to hear; we appreciate your honesty within self to be expressed.

YES, we agree in this offering that to view of this body or thinking apparatus as different in what it has been, seen or heard in what feels like an eternity, than it is to offer that much truth is spoken of here. For one has thoughts and conditions, fears, beliefs, complaints, and sayings to speak from within to feel and these recognitions are so often entrenched within in such a hardness or directness to the defining of what it is that one thinks, sees, or assumes themselves to be.

Does one not?

THIS YOU ARE TO KNOW;

'YOU ARE NOT ALL THIS EARTHLYNESS THAT DEFINES YOU'.

We see as not in this aspect of self to view, for you are in a constant state of change to experience everything and all that appears for you to be witness of. In one's ability to be limited shall we say as to of what it appears to be before them to be seen as an interpretation in a way to express this that they think to see, then they will falter to be witness to many different possibilities, opportunities, or offerings to be seeing into. One must partake in a willingness to want to feel a difference in thought as to what they would normally assume to see and to think we would suggest as a first forward movement to become of this more that is yours to see yourself into or as. In the difference of speak to be partaking into and by this we mean choose words to focus your descriptions of self into as to be desired and daring. Be willing to focus upon all words or thoughts as they are to be offered to be in a responsive attitude to recognise in those that do not build confidence or encouragement from you to feel of.

Let all words or offerings that do not feel as correct or in your liking to hear, be laid down to rest shall we say, as no longer a wanting for you to hold onto. It is in one's willingness to do this to speak of that they must.

I have heard similliar offerings before! Why have I not responded?

It is in only a deliberate intent from within to rise to be spoken, to ask, to question, to search for this new way in which to see of your external seeing's and relationships in regard to self to be held into that one will feel to be in a place of acceptance to be forthcoming from within, to desire a change or movement to be felt within to hope for this to be seen as a timely offering to be responding to.

You are only in your willingness to become of this new way in which it is to think within your so requesting of it to be placed. Judge not here of the all that you have become up to and into this relevant moment of your time.

> *You are willing to change, to hear a difference. Are you NOT?*

This inclination must come from you, not another to speak words as such to you to be in a need to become more than you see yourself as.

Ones thoughts are immensely powerful in this body of containment that you are and in these words that you witness and express every moment of your so choosing of them to become apparent as to whether you are or you are not, will be spoken as gospel to hear as your truth.

Change is required in a sensing of to think, to speak that YOU ARE.

We are always a willingness to be sensed from within this that you are. We are you in a completeness to be felt as us to be you. In this to be spoken we are always forthcoming to the unravelling that one is to feel like this is to hit them with uncertainty, mistrust, or deceit from the one that has held them captive shall we say {meaning you} as to the way in which it was or has been to appear in your world.

To feel like I need to erase all that I thought I am or was, is a difficult notion to get my head around

Is it not?

YES, one would say to this if you have been constantly negating of this worthiness or confidence to say being seen as you are to shine, then yes, it will feel like a challenge to most if not all that see of themselves as NOT.

By allowing of you to feel free to feel and see yourself in a truthful way, to acknowledge of all that you are in this present moment as not of what it is that you must see yourself as but rather an experience or a justification into a thinking way to see yourself as this that you have chosen to get you to this place of recognition of **WHAT** and **WHO** you are.

It is the cause of this stirring to be opened often into a rawness to be seen expressed from you. You are to be reluctant it is to appear to will for or want change to become, for often the fear, pain, and unwillingness that one sits into is safer to feel to know than to contemplate change.

IS IT NOT?

CHAPTER TWO

OUR CONFIDENCE IS YOURS TO MIRROR

Confidence is a word, thought or feeling to offer here to think of that the many of you are too shy to display or even contemplate as to be yours willing to see. One must reject the image of or meaning of confidence as you would know of it to be seen by you within another. For many that display this way of which it is to describe of them to appear, we see roughens or grates upon your very own ego shall we say as to what it is that you think in regard to this word to be meaning to you. Confidence is to be allowing of oneself to be heard from within in your very own unique voice. This voice does not need to be shouted or offered to another in any way other than for you to hear as a confidence within yourself to hear. Confidence as we see it to offer is a belief that is within oneself to be able to see self as the one to be in the knowing of who and what it is that you really are. Confidence is to be displayed in your external actions of self to be seen to participate into this life that you be. Belittled by no thoughts or of others interpretation of you to be, for they do not need to see you as you do this way, and we offer this is okay. You are your own confidence to bring to the table shall we say, and it is often only in the egotistical sense of confidence to be seen from another that one feels to be agitated or grated upon by of what it is that they are to see.

Let all that display this confidence be felt through you as an encouragement from you to be felt not necessarily to be voiced in words, but to be welcomed seeing within this one to present to you as a sense of either self-worth if seen in the correct way, or a decided way from within this human form to think of self as not enough so that one must sprout this egotistical confidence in this way as to appear. You be the decider of your own confidence and deliberate way in which it is that you shall see it to appear from another, you are the true feeler of all emotions and sensing to be yours within, so you will this we say know in truth the real confidence that one is to display when it comes from a balanced soul, or even a beautiful being of love to present to you an honest heart that it speaks to flow from, to the other side of the coin shall we say to the person that feels to boast that they have, are and will. In their belief's it is okay to offer to them a willingness to let all that you see simply BE.

In a deliberate belief within to be allowing one to see of self in this confident way, one shall know to feel that love is directional and intentional into all that it shall be of witness to upon the feelings of this intent to be allowed to be opened or investigated into as of a want to feel.
IS IT NOT?

YOU ARE THE HOLDER OF ALL THAT
THIS IS TO BE SPOKEN OF IN
CERTAINTY OF WHICH IT IS.

YOU ARE THE BEARER OF THIS TO BE
FOUND WITHIN YOU TO CARRY.

YOU ARE THE ONE THAT IS TO HAVE
PLACED THIS REQUEST TO KNOW
WITHIN IN THIS TIME TO SPEAK.

YOU ARE THE BELIEVER WITHIN THIS
THAT YOU HOLD CONFERENCE WITH.

YOU ARE THE ONE THAT IS TO KNOW
CORRECTNESS IN ITS REAL WAY.

YOU ARE THE BODY OF RICHNESS THAT IS
EVER PRESENT IN THE ALL THAT YOU BE.

We have many offerings for you to see yourself as the more that you desire to see yourself as. In this we offer that one must be willing if not even just a tiny inclination to feel. Eliminate the inability to not be allowing to see self in a more-ness to reveal out of this truth that evolved from within you. A sensing of self to explore, to want to know more into these thoughts as they shall arise. We offer there is no right or wrong in a correctness as you would see it to be, it is in this that we wish to establish that your truth is of the most important for you to establish to recognise rising from within. For in this truth all your answers and questions are known.

To will me to be confident, appears challenging to me.

Confidence must not be a want to change. You are you in every correctness that you present yourself to be. To change is to only feel like a hesitation within if it is to grate against your thinking thoughts of this that you appear to be not willing to see yourself as any other thought.

You are a deliberate being into this becoming of and in this notion to feel as a different way to see yourself, you will feel the power of intent that is implanted within you to be deliberately birthed.

So, in this we offer that in deliberate deciding to become you, is the potential within this very essence that you are to be deliberate always into your wanting to be this always. You are the creator of the original confidence that spoke upon your so deciding to be. So, confidence is an alluring notification that is to be strict within you at its best to describe of this to be spoken of, for strength of who and what it is that you are one must be willing to see themselves as this strength needed to stand in a confidence to speak, to think, to hear yourself as a deliberate asker to be always MORE to see.

You are in the eyes that you see, are you not?

How is your view serving you?

You see of all that you are thinking, are you not?

In this limited space to view of self to be is a non-service or an injustice to you to be. One must be diligent into thoughts of or views of this that you are. Be willing to change we say, in only the thinking that you feel incomplete or lost or unable to face another day in this life that you predict to be unliveable. To feel of even the slightest stirring from within is to be called a confidence to be spoke however so hard that one must feel to call of it to be that. You are the holder of all willingness to be spoken of as you to be us in every way.

We sense entirely of you in the words that you speak to hear but we are unwilling to be a wanting to be allowing of us to come to your levels of despair if this is to be a response as such to hear. You are the firm holder of all that you believe in a physical sensation of this human to be. The spirited self, the soul to be yours to be of us is to sense within this to be the speaking of a confidence so bold to speak as hers or his to be that if only just this once you will be in yearning thought to hear....

How does a voice of confidence sound?

Not brash nor booming never to grate upon one's persona of self to be, for this would instantly turn one away from their feeling of confidence to be. In you, you are you, defiantly formed to become. So, allow for the confidence that we see you to be a willingness for you to see yourself always to shine.

Confidence grows rapidly we see to speak of, for in a slight direction to be offered as to the wanting to change for the more to become apparent to be a knowing within that it is more for not always of the others but in yours to be as well.

Change is transformation is it not? Not necessarily transformation but to progress, to further oneself, to become even more, to expand, to be willing, we would offer.

GUIDANCE NEEDED PLEASE:
How to become confident.

> We are not the offerors of anything other than a continuation to see this self through the eyes of complete and instinctual knowing of this to be them in a powerful way 'LOVE'. In the offering of this too many to be felt in the heart space that is to occupy the place that one is to call their physical heart, we are placed directly into with such an intention to be felt upon your so choosing of it to become yours to feel. So, when one is to allow for themselves to feel of this love to begin to speak, one is to sit back a little outside from the thoughts of this to be to know that this is the change, the allowing, or expansion, or deliberate intent from within to

be offered to you to feel your sense of worth
in love of self to be a new way to speak of
this as a confidence that dwells within me.

You are the confidence holder are you not?

It is not delivered ever by another and
in this we say they try, in comments to
feel good by you in a deliverance to be
offered. But often in the non-seer of self
to be this that they speak, it will fall upon
deaf ears to hear. So, in a willingness to
allow for these comments to be yours,

YES, you will try but until the real unfolding
from within this you that you be, until
this big love that you are holder of is to be
accepted as yours and yours alone, until you
can describe yourself as bold of voice to speak
your truth, until you let the sleeping giant
be awakened, then it is that in this process
to get you to the rising of this confidence
to be yours to whole heartedly say.......

'THIS IS I'.

Then we offer; you will feel to struggle and sway, decided into a conviction of this to be not from another as yours to know. For it shall not be offered by these that you see as to love you in a sensing of this to be. You shall always and only want of this confidence to be yours to say to you to feel of this way. YOU are in this place to be present here to say>>>>>

I AM CONFIDENCE IN ALL WAYS
I SEE MYSELF TO BE.

{REPEAT THESE WORDS IF YOU WILL}.

OUCH!! Difficult to speak, we ask?

No one has ever offered this to me to be heard like this before. Why?

Over time much is offered to be heard but it is not, it must come from a willingness in this that you be, to be allowing of such a space to be open within you to feel of yourself to be in an awareness to hear. Vulnerable this may make you feel, but a sense of committing to only you, will prevail.

We are not new to this way in which it is to hear the many of you to speak in yourselves to be thinking of one as. We are the ever listeners or interpreters to all that is expressed to know as your lack of or wistfulness to be this that you are not.

So, in this we are to only offer here to say that we see you only in this way to be the confident illuminating light that you are to beam to the exterior of this human to be, and in this light, we see you always in a willingness to know of this that you are the one, the only one to be.

We sense of you to be sitting on the fence shall we say, as too what it is that you now have heard/ or read.

Often the commitment within this that you are to be offering in as a want to change or believe into, is something that has not come easy to this form that you are to have seen self as before. This in turn then creates much hesitation, resistance, angst or mental walls to be placed in regard to an acceptance as this to see self into. And often it is one that you will fight internally and externally at times to be of a want to see or solve this as a truth that you believe into. All that is to transpire from us to you is in a willingness to hear, is it not? Once contact with the inner being, this loving voice, this blossoming of self is seen, she will be the offeror of this truth to become a stronger version of all truths that you have held onto as yours in an unwillingness it seems to dispel as not correct or maybe not in a need to be yours to think as. You are sitting on the fence shall we say out of fear to disagree with implanted beliefs by existing loves and this fear inhabits this you, blinding you so one cannot see yourself to be of. And in these beliefs, one is unwilling to drop the façade of untruths that they have held about themselves for what is to seem like eternity. It then appears harder to commit to the jumping off the so-called fence and to land heart first into this that be known as self-love to you to be felt. Commitment within oneself to want to change views or words or thoughts are so required here in this that you sit.

Let us offer you a few moments of hesitation here if one needs to express WHY! is it that she/ he will not jump off the fence or walk through the door to call of it that...

Acceptance is yours in your true defining from within to know of this to be yours or not, to be the receiver in you as a truth of yours to hear.

We are willing to wait, for it is not of time that we are concerned by. You are this absolute that you are in this very moment of exactness to feel this need to rest or hesitate, and this is your truth to be seeing as whether it is of yours to need it to be.

MANY OFFER ME SUGGESTIONS IN WHAT I AM TO THINK OF YOU TO BE.

{Authors thoughts}

My thoughts to offer myself as this receiver of all that presents to me to be heard as my truths from in this space of legitimate love that I am to feel as mine to be awash within. And to feel this genuineness that is mine to experience in this my heart and now to speak with those of the all that are to be my ever-continual guiders of this love that I am to be them in all I see.

YOU MAY OFFER WORDS HERE OF YOUR OWN TO BE YOUR SUGGESTIVE THOUGHTS OF HOW IT IS THAT YOU SEE or FEEL SPIRIT, SOURCE, GODS VOICE, DELIBERATE LOVE, or INTERNAL EXPRESSION WITHIN:

However you choose to speak, to recognise or connect is in your truth to do so, in this we are.

....
....
....
....
....
....
....
....
....
....
....
....

CHAPTER THREE

MY OFFERING TO YOU

IN THESE WORDS, I FEEL COMPELLED TO WRITE.

I AM to offer my experience here it appears as to be my interjection of the human and most importantly it seems as to be the writer that receives of these messages in LOVE.

Authors contribution:

YES, I WAS willing to jump off the fence, to open the door and walk through the doorway, shall I say. Not straight away, it took some time to convince myself if I should or not and even why!! was uttered. What have I got to lose was my final response, adding to the feelings of overwhelming from within to find this allowing to be mine?

I was ready, willing, and desiring for more.

I have been one of these humans to speak as to be felt experiencing a rumbling within that grows so uncomfortable to be living in my own skin {shall I say as a representation of how uncomfortable this wanting to know...... **Who and What it is that I AM,** to become}, as it was to present from what appeared to be out of nowhere? Yes! you may feel this as yours to express. Yet...... secretly I knew of its existence for what had seemed like my whole entire life as lived thus far. I was as you maybe are placed in your now; just going about my own business, living this life as best I could. I felt, yes to offer days or moments of self-regret as to wanting to be more, even asking selfishly I thought on many occasions.

There must be more than this, is there not?

And I am assuming you have as have I, read your fair share of self-help, brain enquiry, spiritual understandings, explored different modalities to surround this that I thought as intuitiveness or spirit to represent, whatever I could get my hands on really, I read. I craved what was to be spoken and written. I listened to audios and this also includes the many people that I have spoken to along my way.

Here I am to say; my discovery of this that I am in today, I feel no different in this place of this that I am to be speaking to you as you would be feeling as I was to begin. Maybe lost is too strong a word to offer to some, but it sure feels this way when you begin to be, does it not?

I will also add here that in the thinking that you finally are getting somewhere, more is to rise out of your questions or from connection to sit deeper within in a meditation session or AHA!! moment or an offering that is to grip you with such a conviction to believe into that you research and ask some more.

So, NO the answer here is to offer that your search if to call it that will or is to never end. One is always on this quest for more to be seen, felt, found, and heard. So, embrace every aspect of this so-called journey of yours to cherish into a completeness as yours to progress into, galivanting along as ever the inquirer of self to become.

Spirit or source {allow the name or suggestion be yours to freely speak} and by this let these words to describe of this contentment that is and will be yours before too long to experience as the greatness within you that you will discover again and are to realise that you simply have just forgot.

It will find you this I guarantee.

It is not easy let me say, lots of self-work, intentional receiving, diving deep and opening a rawness and honesty to be accepted by you. And finding a determination to progress into another state of mind or newer, broader thinking ability is the one that I found I struggled with.

What is wrong with me, am I going crazy, why now? I should just drop all this nonsense and go back to being me.

Ahhh! easier said than done right. I hear many of you to agree, for once this initial inclination is to appear as to be yours to notice it is too hard to just forget or put back on the shelf shall we say. It just seems impossible to ignore this opening from within that has captured your attention as to being more than what you appear to be. You are maybe thinking GOSH here we go again another self-help guru trying to offer her way to me. Incorrect I say, for it was mine to discover in this way to be of a realising from myself within that we are all to discover this that is yours to speak of in this way as yours not mine. Yes, I have suggestions and stories of my own to be shared, maybe they will appear as another writing to receive to be written, but for now it is to be spoke that spirit, your inner guidance and in this they are not fussy shall I say to be expressed in any particular way as your words of them. Take note; the important step is the heart that you hold so divinely within that craves of you to feel this from within as yours to experience, so that in the day that we shall meet I will be ever willing within myself to hear of your acceptance of this that is explained by me as my SELF-LOVE to become the ever-intuitive receiver to see of the all that I be known into as the love that is unconditionally mine to be accepting of.

Let these words of encouragement be yours to fall into, to know that this journey as one would explain it to you to be hers. That she (meaning myself) has felt many tears well & fall, I have lost what I thought to be loving, caring, and understanding friends and family along the way in my quest to be this exactness that I was surely to become. The depths and darkened states of my revealing's explained as grand and not, have been to my advantage I would suggest this as my unravelling, my discovering, my learnings of all that I am and shall continue to be considered an evolving of this ME. There is still much work that I need to do to become for it is never ending this experience to grow I say, one is to leave all ego and attempts to be seen as not humble outside before she is to enter. For in the true discovering of the all that you thought was dear and right within you, you may feel as I did, a disrespect in the viewing of the not so to be and in the beliefs that I thought I was. All these suggestions/ or mistruths will rise in a certainty for you to express in a forgiveness it is to appear, you must.

I shall offer here to say that you are on the correct path no matter how confusing it is to feel, for this is the way in which it was to discover all uncertainties that you are, no path is ever without its ups and downs, is it?

Describe to me of what it is that you see I have been often asked and asked of the many that I have interpreted their journey as my own. A level of jealousy or contempt rose often within to be not hearing as they appeared to do. I was often told that I myself was not. This I rebutted and felt disruption within overtake me. My feelings to be thinking that I was trying hard to see, hear and become. Surely, I was, was I not?

The truth to be spoken of here was YES it was that I was not hearing, but it was not of spirit that I was to hear just yet, it was to be ME in an honesty and truth of self to recognise and feel this heart of mine to speak unashamedly and in a rawness never heard before by me, and in here it was that I was to know deeply and honestly myself before I was to hear anything else. And it was not until this relationship with ME began and still does continue to this day that we speak, I know now that it was too soon to be. Now on my timing of it to be so called to the surface to recognise in the defiant truth that it was written as mine to be heard. In this I offer to you that we are all implanted with such a desire of this to become ours to know{remember} and that you will as I did to feel my opening/awakening as to the all in and of spirit to be this benevolent truth within me, and in your time to be yours to have written for it to be yours.

IT SHALL.

Much is previewed and experienced in the many moments of self-analysing and introspection of this human that I am to appear to myself and you to be, I searched inwardly and externally in many hours of meditation, journaling, speaking to those that I thought held the truth. This I soon discovered they did not for me, nor did the hours I wasted if to appear to be this to speak of about the times I sat in an unwillingness to be hearing this voice that I was to discover to be mine, so loving, so patient, so truthful to be giving to me all that I was needing to hear. I am to carry this one with me as my own intuitiveness that stands correct within me. Trust these words that I offer, you carry one of your own to be seen as exactly this your truth wrapped beautifully within, it is always as mine is attached in completeness to these that I have said in many conversations to my guides, my reflections of self, my space of peace and quiet that I adore of the all that presents to me in a willingness to accept of what is right for me to be the recipient of in this time. Your timing is explicit and correct within you this I say, and yes I will offer to you that I did get very impatient in times of many to be receiving more and asking of this to be bestowed upon me to see more, to hear and feel more. WHY impatient? you ask, if you are to be just in what one would feel the place of this opening to start, hear my words to speak that you will become impatient, eager, and even inspired to be seeing more, feeling more, asking more as this that is correct within you to feel. You are of the same place you and I, this I have discovered in the allowing of myself to hear not only my truth to be but know of yours to be just this that I see in me. I know of all that we are to be together is in a unity of self and beings alike to become once again this divine intervention of the real love that we possess within to be ever sitting into a magnificence of TRUTH and LOVE to become once again.

I can say this in truth; that my love that I have discovered that is mine is very real to feel and if you were to ask am I still the same person that I was before I discovered this, I am not sure of what it is to be called in a human understanding other than a love so deeply implanted into this very essence of who it is that I am. My answer would be definitely NO for one is to grow and grow and when she thinks that she cannot grow no more you will feel as though you are dumped, tumbled, and stripped bare again to speak, and to realise, remember and learn that there is always more to this interpretation of spirit, source, god, the one, the allowing within your words to be spoken of as yours to see into.

Be bold I was to be in this offering to write and of this I did with hesitation in my heart as some of you may know. But bold I chose to become this truth that I am, always in a yearning to see me in the ones that are to grace your dreams, thoughts, heart life to be known as yours to experience in your own way and not through or out of another's experience to be. This is your wanting to become you in this place in time and so it shall be this YOU that you see.

CHAPTER FOUR

GROWING INTO THIS EXPERIENCE

In here we see you as you blossom so profusely into a becoming of complete belief into this that you be.

Becoming this certainty to hear oneself as she/he is to speak.

Feelings of contentment that are to warm you from within this physical sensation that you are.

Drive and decisions as they were intended to be yours to want, to see, to feel.

This realising to be at one with self and in a resting to see all that are themselves to be.

You will feel this flow of contentment to be yours to offer to self as newfound confidence into this very interpretation of this self to be YOU.

'THE BEAUTIFUL YOU WITHIN ME'

You are deliberate in this self to speak, are you not?

We are to sense no fear or hesitation as it is to progress for you along this path of self-awareness or SELF discovering as you are all willing to call this experience of life upon this planet to be.

Let us offer here in this time as yours to hear that this lifetime is filled with many interventions and expectations into what it is that one thought or imagined themselves to be by now it appears as we speak. Let go of all these tightening's and constrictions to think that you did not, will not or wont, for this is the wrong assuming that one must take. Let us say you arrived here did you not? YES, willingly we heard you speak; not without some trials and tribulations along my way though.

That is okay to verbalise and take ownership for. They were yours; yes, we are to hear you say, in a forgiveness to yourself to be wanting to witness a generosity within to be felt as a sense of release. You are not responsible for those that served you wrong or did wrong by you, but you are responsible in your thoughts of yourself to be held into these many situations that you feel as to have or should have handled in a different way. Were you or not meant to? We ASK?

Learnings, teachings, growth, development of soul happens in the exactness that it was presented to be your experience as and in this we say feel a softening within to see yourself as not to have been strong enough or certain enough or bold enough to withstand these feelings of grief, rejection, self-harm, or abuse that you felt drawn to as yours to experience.

All is correct within your world if you are to see it in your internal eyes of forgiveness towards you to be accepting as a willingness to be just this perfection in this your here and now to speak.

Do not dwell or linger into the past we say as a levering to the want and was of what it was. You are not in that now you are here in this to be your ever present NOW, the place of solace to be found within in the asking of this newfound confidence to be seen as yours to step into to accept with no attachments to be felt needed.

Feel compelled from within to grow, you must.

In just this simple statement to be made or suggested it is to feel of an encouragement to come forth from within to be heard.
Does it not?

You are the one who is willing to be the asker of this change, this growth, this expansion, or new direction to be seen by you. If one is to be the asker of this new becoming to be a sign of a willingness to spring forth from your thoughts to be asked by you, even if just for a moment to contemplate a newness to be discovered by you, then you will.

In the seer that sees of self as not to be responsive or in a decision shall we say to see of the person as you to be not wanting to move forward or even open to a slight suggestion from within to be looked into, then in this we say you will. If you are witness to the voice of love that is within you to be heard, then you will at least try. Let all resistance to the thinking mind be of this that you are not, and just take a leap of undying faith in self to be felt as to be the asker to experience something new.

- ❖ I will with intent speak of myself only in this new way to view or speak of myself to be. I know that I Am willing to be aware of the all that I am to hear and see myself to be, in this I acknowledge that this is okay.

- ❖ I am considerate of my own needs in this time it appears to ask to be kinder, more caring and allow for myself to be knowing of intentional time to focus upon me.

- ❖ I am willing to hear all that is spoken by me in this voice that is love for myself.

- ❖ I embrace all this that I think or see to be wrong or not enough in me, this is okay.

- ❖ I am willing to respond to my thoughts with a compassionate heart.

- ❖ I forgive all thoughts that I have carried into this moment of self-reflection.

We can add many more statements like these so mentioned, but it is to offer here that one must be willing to hear oneself speak in such caring words to be said by themselves to feel as though they can or even are willing to express change towards a growing from within to be seen into.

'You are all this deliberate knowing that is you in an essence of purity that you all possess to be eternal love within, show yourselves that you believe into yourself again to know that this is you'.

BE ready to accept all of you, ready to experience sensations of self-respecting love for yourself, ready to grow steadily into a new way to express, ready to hear a voice that is not the one that you normally hear to listen, ready to flourish from within to watch, ready to feel as this form that you are appears to change, ready to release any guilt/ or hurt that I still carry in regard to this disappointment that I saw myself as, ready to demand a certainty to be spoken by you into the direction that you know is yours to see, ready to accept this new you to be the you that you want to hear and see more of, ready to explore all possibilities with an open mind and sense of allowing yourself to do so, ready to watch in fascination as all people> places >objects and situations become an awareness around you like you have never witnessed before, ready to explore yourself in many different scenarios and conversations and hear your voice speaking boldly to hear as this decidedness within you to trust in your truth, ready to connect, ready to allow for all that present to you to be perfect in their own expectations of this that they are, ready to allow for ones voice to be heard in a perfect unison as yours to be this that we are to speak boldly within you, ready to embrace this love as unconditional and mine to be, ready to be loved by me, ready to be love, ready to be ready, I AM READY...

I AM.

*I feel change
emerging,*

I AM READY in all that I am to be.
I let no one or any other be the
change that I need to see in me.
I am in a contemplation of this to
become it may appear at times but to
be willing I say is a benefit of mine.
I am prepared to be guided directly
from within, to hear my voice as it has
never been said. Confident and proud
of this very being I am as I stand here.
Maybe not for you to see me but
allowing of myself to see me.

I am gracious of heart in the
all that I feel me to be.

I am closed off to some this
it appears, but not to me.
I am drawing closer to myself each
day, closer to the one that I love again,
and I am willing to hear and see.
I am selfish it may seem at times when I
lock myself away or appear to disappear,
but to me this is an eagerness within, only

wanting to see this perfection that I be.
I am guilty of time spent unfocused
or literally wasted it would appear to
some in my time of isolation or solace
it appears to be seen, this is for me
to grow and expand with no other to
suggest on how it is that I should be.
I am wanting my life to be
grand, this I speak.

I am wanting my life to be always more and
feel unashamed to say it in this knowing way.

I am worthy of this and the
all that I can and will be.
I am willing to express my voice
in a boldness to be spoken.
I am willing to trust in this that I am.

I AM changing.......

"I AM"

CHAPTER FIVE

ARE YOU READY? WE ARE.

By ready; do you mean, scared to be me.

If in one's essence of self to be feeling shall we say a nervousness to be oneself to allow for a change of view in perception of self to be asked for, then YES.

We would suggest to the many of you that are willing in this your now to accept an agreeance from this that you are to be the speaker, to say one is to be hesitate yet excited, deliberate yet nervous. These are all human emotions attached to a fear or uncertainty within that one has been forever arguing with and about the wanting to feel a change within to be seen, Is it not?

You are the truest version of you that we see and let us offer here that in the holder of this bolder, braver version of you that you are within maybe at your own demise as to never have seen or heard. Let us offer; she is coming for you?

To be the asker to see or question oneself as to be thinking differently into almost all aspects of this human being that you are is the initial step to progress into.

You have been doing deliberate work within yourself, have you not?

Of this we ask because it is in our truths to know that you have. You have got to this definite place of being because you have chosen of this to be yours to realise as you.

You are equipped with such a magnificence from within that is your most secret admirer to date. One has maybe shown just a little interest or even not been asking of this to become but are feeling movement naturally within. Are you not?

Please give me guidance as of what I shall hear, see, or knowing what to ask.

This we have heard many times over by those of you that are choosing shall we say in your words to awaken. To feel of this stirring from within it has been offered as to shake your form within, offered an unsteadiness to your thoughts and speech, it has defiantly rattled your life to the extreme of wanting to know. Has it not?

We be the believer in you to answer YES to this hesitantly it may seem or attached to an unsureness surrounding even what it is that this is to appear as. Why we hear you ask?, it is you evolving, moving, remembering, recognising, loving you in the state that you asked us to be always seeing of you as.

THE REAL YOU IS READY. IS SHE NOT?

We know you are, you have already committed, have you not?

The truth speaker within you, the deliberate speaker within you, the knowing speaker within you has answered you in many attempts in which to be heard. This we know of.

You are always the one that controls this awakening to be spoken of as this in this way that we see you becoming the real version of you, the one that stole our hearts shall we say upon your entering into this reality of which it was that you became.

Your shine has broadened our smiles if it was to be offered as a suggestion to you to receive you as this in our lovingness that we see you all as complete. You have revisited this day many times over and over of this uniqueness of yours to be willing and confident to be exposed. So, how does it feel to be here finally?

ARE YOU READY FOR MORE?

Can you ask for more than of this that you are already to see yourself as and to have so far.

YES, YOU CAN, AND YOU WILL.

To be this deliberate intent to be held within, you are the ever receiver of more, more to you is exactly as it is to feel like for you to interpret it to be. Never be shy again to ask, dream, envision or imagine oneself as more or too have more. This was, is and always will be the place of instant attraction to the receiving of this that one is to ask. IN here it is that your heart has flung open, it feels free again to love, and be loved by you and to see us within as your soul, spirit, and grace. It is of this feeling to transpire into that one must admire within herself/himself to see, for you did this in a willingness to realise of your truest potential that you hold within.

THANKYOU FOR YOUR PERSISTANCE,
we say.

You should be immensely proud in yourself and the progress that one has made.

We hear you say that you feel like you are only just to begin.

In this we say that for some of you, this may be true. But in these pages of script to be received so far, we offer, we have seen a willingness, maybe even a want or curiosity to be present to read more, to request to know more, to hear more. HAVE YOU NOT?

So, allow for this very present moment of your so-called time to connect, hear, feel, or read these words, give way to allow yourself permission to overcome these feelings of doubt to suggest that you are maybe not as far along as the most that you see. This is not for you to fear or reject the possibility to know within that you may be further than you are to think.

Your journeys are all becoming exactly as they were transcribed by your greater good to be spoken of to receive, to see.

So, trust in this magnificent being that you present to us here today to be the one that knows just exactly how far it is that you have become and know this that we speak that you are correct in your presence to be present, right NOW.

Your confidence in me is contagious.

We know, it is to be spoken. For you are so genuine in this that you appear to us to be. We see of you all as the many that there are to inhabit this planet to become exactly who you are. We fear not to be heard by you for we know you will. It is a feeling that is to run deep within to be felt first this we have spoken, and it is in this feeling of us to be present to feel, sense or hear it is then that we know that we have your attention so far. You are sureness in self it is for us to see, often it has needed a nudge from within or comment or suggestion to have been thrown your way. Our offerings appear along your path of lives in many ways, deliberate some may seem, later to revisit on how it was that we were to have met. Yes, it is in this that we be willing in all our capacity to encourage this self from within this form to be known again for she is the shining light that you be for us to see.

We encourage you in this place that you appear to us to be now, to hear always of this great intent rise from within you to speak. Be honourable to yourself in a want to hear this voice that be yours in ours to speak, encouragement comes thick and fast in this place to feel content. Know that you are ever expanding this we know; more is always of a wanting and this is okay to ask to know. This more is yours in a difference compared to others that ask, this we see. Know that they too will find their more to ask if not the same as yours but different to be spoke.

> *You are unique and original we say, live your life like you know this that you are special to be.*

THERE WE SAID IT. CAN YOU?

> *Maybe quietly for now, but later i will roar.*

We encourage you in this space of us to be a willingness for you to see, to hear, to feel you are the roar from within waiting to present.

Let her roar!!! Do not be shy for you have hid this roar away for way to long it appears to us and those that know you well and have seen this potential inside.

Stand encouraged by your thoughts of this that you have become, for here is your story thus far as we have seen it to be yours. Anxious has crossed your path, doubt has reared its ugly head, disbelief into of what and if we are real or not, self-assessment in the thoughts of how, when and why you should or could be, emotions have drained you, elevated and filled you to no end, struggles to express of what it is that you see within, experiences have come and gone, willingness to commit has and is spoken of in certainty now so in this we say.....

YOU ARE READY TO ROAR.

Quietly or alone if you must but please.... ROAR

CHAPTER SIX

HEAR ME ROAR

Delve into this space with me, for I feel
the readiness within you to speak.

Your words are the same as
mine, are they not.

A wanting to be you in a
completed comparison to none.
We are all the same you and I and the ones
that are to respond to the voices of ours.

Hearing them speak for the very first
time was in our experience to be spoke.
You and I are all the same are we not.
We sit together you and I in unison to be,
deliberate with this intent to be seen.

Our voices are witnessed by
this that we thought as not.
You and I are to be the same are we not.
Inspired by ancient ever giving
wisdom from within.

You and I are this same wisdom are we not.
We speak of a love divine to be felt
as all correct to be within.

You and I are this same divine
love, are we not?

There have been many words offered to hear, Is ROAR the newest?

YES, in this we agree. For you like words to see, to speak and are often attached to the emotions felt as an attitude within you in regard to the sounding or acknowledging of these words to express and to be seen as a vision of yours to except as their meaning to you to be.

ROAR is one is it not? Spoken of to be delivered with a great power, a certainty to be heard, a warning not to get to close, for it is in all of these to suggest that it is a word that one is to attach to loudness and intensity to be seen, heard, and even felt as a vibration from within in its willingness to feel of its intent.

ROAR we say, let it out, let it be heard.... you know you want too!! GREAT!! Well done.... now then let us explain. You have been the one that has remained quiet to others, including yourself in your voice to speak, have you not?

It is the many of you here in this comment to ask to read, that we speak as an ever knowing from within this that you partake into as a willingness to be given permission shall we say as to let it all fall outwardly to be spoken by you as your voice of recognition into this that you knew. You have always been intuitive or assessing of thy self and others or situations that you have been present within, have you not?

You have always been curious as to the what and ifs that could or should have been, Have you not?

You have always held back these words of love and encouragement to yourself and others to be spoke, have you not?

We see many if not most of you to feel these statements as they are read as to the wanting that has burnt this desire from within you to be seen to be felt as the real you in a wanting so deep to be recognised as you to be this voice that speaks in your truth and not of another ever again.

My voice has always been mine has it not?

To answer this in an honesty for us to receive as yours to ask us to answer. WE shall.

We have witnessed many of you to presume that this voice that you have spoken has been yours to a certain degree. But in this we are to offer how many times of past have you agreed or spoken in an understanding or voice of another to be interpreted as yours to hear yourself speak. This we say has elapsed out of a lack of worthiness to be felt to hear or a fear of others and their decisions or thoughts of such to be theirs, lack of confidence to know that you are the correct within that one must see. There are many deliberate intentions here that are to lay within you to think that you have voiced your way successfully we see and in this we say yes you have, because this voice that you have spoken into and of has been your voice up until now to have been the only one that you are to have known.

MY VOICE IS BOLDER THAN I REMEMBER.

We would be accepting of this to receive as a comment by you to think it to be.

But one must be reminded here to say that yes, your voice appears bolder or louder or more determined to be heard as this that you seem to hear it as, only in the acceptance by self to feel more confident, more complete, and more willing to accept and to speak this of you as more the truer version of you. You have grown, expanded into this voice of choice shall we say to be yours to become into a willingness to know the more of you, have you not?

We are always to offer this in response to how it is that one feels around this suggestion of bold, loud, and willing to speak for them to hear as this. You are the speaker of truths to be yours. So in this; one will feel a certain resistance to apply these words in a descriptive reasoning to be yours felt. In your willingness to have found a deeper sense of love within you, a love that is so bold in its unfolding once found as yours to be related to, it is in this loving voice that you become the louder, bolder, and more loving version of you to sit. So, in this we suggest to you that your knowing of these words to you to be seen in this way as contentment, encouragement, and desire of yours to be, will and shall remain.

To be willing to speak bold feels like a defiantness within, should it?

All that have held back from the discovery of the intentional you within will feel this to stir often shall we say. It has always been within you this voice of bold to be spoken of in this way for you to hear. This is your encouragement to become YOU....

In the timing of it to be allowed to be previewed one will often feel a hesitation surrounding this suggestion from us to you to be seen into as a place of which it is to ask,

HOW LONG HAVE YOU HIDDEN YOUR VOICE AWAY, WE ASK?

Your opinions or internal thoughts or offerings are yours to be made to self-first and foremost, it is not to feel as though another needs your thoughts as words to be offered by you. In confidence to grow you will feel as your certainty within in all that you think to know and feel about yourself in this that you are and you will feel the need to be heard in a correctness in which it is that one will speak her truth. Be not limited we say by always to feel as in need to correct another by words of yours to offer, for they are correct in their own right it is to be seen, with no justification or correction by you needed to speak. If of what it is that they are to say, appears to irritate or feels incorrect for you, walk away. You are in your right to be happy within self to not let another drag you into their bubble of discontentment accessing you in how they interact. Feel as you are righteous enough in this new discovery to be this voice that speaks your truth of bravery and courageous love for you to be heard.

BE BOLD WE SAY.

Being bold scares me, especially when I see it present in another.

"Let their bold be theirs" in this simple statement it appears to be theirs to speak, does it not?

It does not have to be your version of bold. In meaning we are all to see within you, the realness that you be for you. We see all of you as bold in no uncertain way shining deliberately as the creator of self to become so bold to us in intention, it is to see for you all to stand into. So, may we suggest that to turn a deafened ear or take a silent approach to show will enable all of you that feel this boldness of another to be to direct to be softened in ones thoughts to think that it is just their wanting to be seen, to be heard by all that they interact with as in need of being present within themselves to be.

You are the deliberate hearer of all that you hear, let your brave voice of intuition and wisdom of such as how it shall be understood as your bold to be for you, your roar is unique.

PLEASE, let it be!

Easier said than done we hear you say.

You are the holder of this voice as we see it to be. Sit into this space of recognition of us to be, a simple understanding of a willingness to be heard, a breathe to inhale and then to deliver out, a longing to connect, to interact in this space of peace and calm to be, a moment of self-intent to be felt from within, a passage of your time to be quiet to resist of all that appears external to see. These are a few suggestions of placement to become yours to hear your voice again over and over as new to be spoken by you.

You are the version of you that was to become. So, the sooner that you acknowledge this within self to hear that this is you, the easier this viewing will be. Now take a look at how far you have travelled without a preview of self in a lacking view but in a way to preview as 'WOW' look what I choose to learn, to experience, to discover, to expand into to be here in this very moment of my present now.

We see of you in many to sit so often in despair it would feel to us to see this to be yours to experience into for such of a wanting of self to be seen differently from another view and self-respecting thoughts within self to be. Allow for yourself to hear this now that you are okay within this one to speak to know that this is you. Deliberate one must be and wanting to hear your sweet voice for love to be heard by you.

It is a topic that we preview repeatedly in many ways as which it is to be spoken of or written about.

This limiting factor or flaw that we see too often in these ones that are choosing to speak, from the very moments of your conception it is to appear upon one a suggestion of thoughts and attitudes to be thrust upon this trusting soul spoken as to by another. You are guided by many in a focus of theirs to so choose. They are honest and caring for most but feel the need to intend upon you their opinions, belief's, thoughts as theirs to be your own.

If one could take lots of care here to hear as this to be their own that they must be wary of all that speak to you as to even consider it for yours to be responsive to, one should not. You are your own decider? Correct! In what is to sound right or not within for you. One must be respectful of all that place a presentation of speech before you to say, in this let it pass to you then through you in no sense as a responsibility to be held as yours to think or respond to if not needed to be felt as yours to hear. You will begin to filter more of you, as not your thoughts in this to be of another to be, but in you this we suggest as the right way to be.

All are important in their own voice to hear this is right, but you are the one that is more important to hear as correct within.

It is time to drop the pretence that you over time have not been willing to see this roar as your own. We sense the willingness to become a real speaker of your truth to be yours.

You are to ask of this in no uncertain way as to be heard by you in every day, every moment of self to be this that you are.

We are to roar from within if truth be told for once you are felt to have unravelled or unfolded the you that we see hidden away by this dimmed version of light that you are, it is in this instance of self-recluse to be willing to step forward and to shine like she was intended to be seen. Then in this very moment of your now to exist that you must feel the roar to interrupt all that you think yourself to be spoken of in such way, let it escape, this deliberate noise from within, a yearning to begin to roar to the outer-ness of all eternalness that you be, YOU.

CHAPTER SEVEN

DISCOVERING THIS NEW SELF TO BE ME

She has always been there to interpret as
yours to see of to know.
Never has she been hidden from us to be
witness too.
It has been in your apparent state of which
it was to view that you have been blind to the
viewing of her to be.
She has forsaken and forgiven all suggestions
as not to be heard or seen as her to be.
She has laid willingly within this that you be.
She is the founder of your light to be shining
as yours to see.
She will always be your encouragement
from within to be the discoverer
of the NEW SELF to be.

You are the founders of this that you be, and your becoming was a choice that one was to have made to become. You say all your wisdom as correct within to be spoken for the eternalness that you were and are to become. In this we see of you in this place of despair to be not feeling the encouragement from within to be yours to see yourself in a place of which it appears not to receive. Follow this guidance as it is to be placed before you to hear as your own in sensing of it to be right within you to feel. For our words are of many that are choosing this here and now to be spoken. It is of you that we see unique and complete in this form. You are explicate in the divinity that is to rule supreme within you, to be an asset to us if one is to explain it in this way. 'You are the obvious choice here that you made to see this as your own to see yourself to be'. Feel as you are to find some form of encouragement no matter how small it is to appear for this is the human understanding into of how one is to grow to expand. Deliberate intent from within to hear of this wee voice, willing and very capable to become a loud roar. So, to see of self in this new 'ME' way is to only know of this as the way that you became, NEW to this earth it would appear deliberate in this form to be, but know of this it is here that you have been before in another succession of self to be. Noticed by many it is this that you are deliberate to one that is all that you are in need to be and this one is you and the one that we be within you to always be seen as you, needing to see the NEW YOU that you are already being.

Spirits offering: We are deliberate in this intent to be received by this one that appears to speak these loving words to be received as her own, to be the voice that one must be decided to hear as her own. We are to be in a space of which it appears to be in an offering for the all if not most of you to hear this that we speak.

Your real exsistance speaks loudly here.
{We are to offer}.

You have been in this space before you know, one of incoherent understanding of self to grow, a realisation that has grown from within this space to be yours to reach out to become. An explicit understanding of self was made as a deliberate attribute to determine as yours again, maybe out of an asking that you made intentionally in human form or not. But your inner guidance has spoken with you a lot intuitively or by natures understanding in this you were to understand. You have stood before us in many times to be seen and able to express of this that you have chosen to become. To grow into a succession or progression of this light as this soul within to be seeing of the possibilities and potential that she/he has willingly chosen as hers or his to become.

So, you see the greater the chancing of this that we are to meet is more correct within than that you are to know than of what it may appear to be so in this your present now to express. Let all inhibitions regarding this self as to not know, be laid to rest for you are just the containment of something far greater than you will ever know and she/ he is the one, ever continual to be upon this journey that you shall meet to know as the reasoning behind the all that you do and do not know.

Growing bolder in every instance that she/ he is to present, training into this becoming as ever continual, ever learning to become as one with thy self to progress even further into this expansion that we shall offer to you to hear as yours.

It is to appear that if one is to let these selections of words settle in, to be received as truthful guidance from this that we be seen from above to be yours to comprehend that you are this that you wished of self to become. Let all resistance lay, throw caution to the wind, and ask this to be yours in a willingness to try. For you are the exactness in this your now that you have chosen to become. Do not be deterred by these words or writings to have read. For if one is to feel a connection within to rise, know that the powers that be so focused within this that you are, the ones that steer your boat shall we say, we are the commander of your ship to help you navigate your decisions as to your How's and Whys. So in these simple words one must be willing to know that they simply just must BE. We have been quoted often to speak, and to know of this as.... *All just 'IS'*.

It is always a challenge it appears for this one in physical appearance to hear these words of simplicity spoken, simply because too much attention is often given upon what it is that one is to have received in a quest to delve in deeper or to hear more to understand. Know it is all given to you this you are to have heard to know in your time space reality of which it shall become.

Why we ask; is it to fight or antagonise over this as more than what it is that you are to receive in this any given moment of you to be. Let all be right and correct within this being to be felt, for you are the newer you, the releaser you, the truer you to be seen in this very moment of present to be yours to see. Always ever changing, ever continual, ever sensing of this willingness that is if she/he is allowed to do her/ his job as designated from you in your so choosing of this to be your voice of wisdom to carry within to be heard as your truth, the true you that you are now here to see.

You are deliberate in your intent to be this. Are you not?

You are progression to succeed into all of which it is to be held into, are you not?

By this we offer up a suggestion to most to see of themselves in a broader way, expel all misconceptions to be only of this that you present to us in this human form.
You are not.

Your abilities to become far outweigh this of what it is that you think of yourself to be more.

You are extraordinary beings of love and eternally a continuation of light to be responsive within. We speak these offerings for the many of you that sit to receive this new concept as spoken by us, to be received by you, to see yourself as this sensor of power that you hold within, and always have been the entitlement of. We see many to explain as ignorant, fearful, or yet unhearing or non- recognising of this awesome power known as yours. *Why we ask?*

Deliberate to be seen by you we have been. You are a continuation of form to be ever expressing within this self as a realisation of something more intentional to become. We speak maybe for some in riddles it appears here to grasp, but trust in your asking this that is maybe still raw, uncertain, even misguided by other's opinions blurring your own acceptance of yourself in this way. Your journey may appear to have just begun but let us interject here in a more constructive way to speak of this beginning as such to be explained.

For many if not all to think of this life as just one, one will struggle to feel an allowance as this information to be correct. You are all growing and expanding within an evolvement of which is us, we sense of one's head to be filled with much interpretation or stories to be told by many in their understandings of this to be true. So, to hear of a deliberate voice to speak in a sensing of this to be true from within you, is often a place of doubt or disbelief to find oneself in. It is not to have you disagree or feel as though you are not being true to you that we speak. It is to be in your own determining, in your so time of which it is that you will speak, that you will hear of these voices once again as yours to be complete. Let us not deter you from this place that one is to sit if not willing to be wanting to hear of us to speak. It is not to deter us in any way or discredit us to those that think of us a completeness within them that will and ever is to be heard as us. You all will find your own way of this as truth within to be found to hear.

CHAPTER EIGHT

FEELING COMMITTED TO THE CAUSE

FIRST, I HAD TO FIND ME.

WHY? YOU ASK.

IN the deliberate attempt to become who I thought that I had to be for the many people that surround me in this very life of my so choosing to find me, or more truthfully be what I thought I had to be for those that I knew.

I know now that this was not me at all.

This is where the search was to begin or so it seems, these words or thoughts became a strong asking of **WHO OR WHAT AM I.**

I, in this lacking that I felt, searching deeply and often into thoughts of this that I was to be the same or similar of the many that I surrounded myself with, or sought to be in company of.

A chameleon I became great at interpreting others and trying my best to fit in.... **Sound familiar.** There was always someone that you wanted to be, wanted to be liked by so and so, or felt limited physically in a sense of multimedia and so attached images that appear, being plastered continually to blunt and dullen our expectations of ourselves.

I was the pleaser, the do-gooder, the non-complainer, the shut my mouth and put up with it, the agreed even when I totally disagreed, the engagement in comments that I disliked, etc etc the list goes on, I felt like I had to be all these things when I really did not wish to be any of them.

Who was I anyway? I began to ask.....

{Authors thoughts + offerings}

Sound familiar, we have all been surrounded by the boasters, the overbearing humans with comments to bold to even consider saying yourself ever, this is not me, the not wanting to be there, the get me out of here, the I dislike what you are saying.... the list goes on and on and I think it is fair to offer that my personal experiences are similar if not the same as many that are to read these pages of script.

The scenarios get worse the further into this journey of allowing oneself not to be loved completely by the most important one ever, and YES this is you.

You are to expel so much energy being something that you are not, speaking words that do not suit you or make you feel uncomfortable, listening to others that are not compatible with you and your way to think. Now we offer here with intent to speak that it is not of those to be seen as wrong in any way, just to explain that they are not of you in an energy exchange, all are present in their so offering as such to be. Leave them if not to feel right, this you will know as not to hurt, disrespect or harm in any way, but to simply be true to you. Yes, it feels like I have never fitted in and let me say I have tried to mould myself to be of this that I thought would.

I was one of those people I am sure and still am at times of uncertainty, even to describe it as a gutless wave to wash over me or that swells from within a sense of doubt and at some point, to observers of me I hold my hand up and say YES, I am guilty on all accounts. But I know the difference is that now I try to not be overwhelmed or caught up shall I say in what I hear spoken or looked upon as to feel no longer to serve me so. Deliberate intent needed here to swerve another way.

Let me say when you are looking to be found, the real you will do anything.

Will she not?

But I can say honestly that now I know this of me to be, that in the finding of me and only this me that I wish to see, not the me that I think or thought that others were needing to see, is where I found this me feeling completely self-assured upon my decision to be just ME.

For the many that I am to witness often and may I suggest that there will always still be comments, situations, stories to tell, greater adventures than mine, more money, better assets, stronger personalities etc etc, than me. In the process of to look deep and unwrap an ability I discovered it is described to me as this 'LOVE of ME'. Allowing of this I must and constantly I am being reminded by myself of how important my inner space and growing within my spiritual practise to sit into was for me by allowing peace and calm into my life. In conversations with my inner presence, {this may be your higher self or internal lover, gods voice or lighthouse however this innerness is recognised by you, is correct for you}.

I found that none of these concerns that I battled with often as to over think or dwell into often being left unresolved or felt as to degrade myself, were not to matter. It is in this trusting space that I became ME, the real ME.

The me that I had searched for and tried continually to become by seeing myself in others and certain situations that were never mine to see into or become

I released.

Are you thinking this story sounds like yours?

I am sure it does if you are to be truthful, I am thinking it would be the greater population that are to feel trapped into this escapism of self to become something that they are not.

We are to suggest here to offer that the many that we see to interpret, are searching furiously to become of this that they are not, nor are they ever meant to be. Let us offer here in this place to give correction of this thinking that you are to search into another to become more. In the doubting initially that is to become when one starts to see of another as better, bolder, wiser, or prettier than, one will start to feel the demise from within that you are to eliminate the owner of this unique form that you are. She/he becomes unjust in conversations within self to be heard and starts to focus on what is not instead of all that is. Let all resistance regarding the wishing to be of this that you are not, be allowed to feel as though it is to become a place of not needed to analyse into. For in your viewing through physical eyes, it is exactly this that you see to be. We are the knowers of this to be a great intention within the human body to ask to be more than they think of themselves to be. Yes, sounds like a contradiction to most but to be caught in a trap of contentment that feels like another's and not your own is to weigh heavy upon ones soul to be spoken of as; to not be hearing your true genius within.

Many are raised and focused on an early interpretation to be ignorant and unhearing to the original self, the born out of love self, the self that is everything already, the self that is to be seen in such this way as to be perfection. In many moments of our so recognitions, we are always privy to other's comments, expectations, beliefs, and stories told, yes, it is apparently a part of the earthly culture to be described as. But one is encouraged here to start to make your own judgements to be yours to only express to self to cherish your decisions that you make, *it is never too late.* See only out of your eyes to love and be persistent in this space daily.

Love more, than judge to hate.

Release slowly if need be, others, including family/friends and their attributes or suggestions to you over many moments of yours to sit into, to hear, to witness to see, let your inner peace be accepting of your responses to the how's and whys they are to suit you or not. For it is not to let them go we offer,{and some may of own accord, this is to be right for them and you we offer} it is to witness though all that present or appear placed upon your path to accept as in their own right to know. Leave well and good alone, trust in the higher power that lives within to be the seer of all that is truth in you and others to see to be the inspiration that they so are needed to be to them. Be bold within this that you are. You are the player of this life, you are the desirer of this self to become, you are the holder of the greatest wisdom within, you are the knower of all that you are, you are the one true interpreter of you.

ARE YOU READY?

Easier said than done, we hear you say.

We have said these words before, repeatedly for ones such as you to hear. Trust us you will, in your time of so choosing of them to be worthy to hear within yourself to want them to be this change or shall we say clearer recognition that you are in need to hear.

We offer these words often and in truth for all to connect into. It is in our doing to know that the many of you will continue to interpret yourself as this to be and are okay with all that you see. Great we say, if you can feel blessed, happy, and content into this that you are to present here in this your now, then we say you are well underway. Your truth is to be your truth we say and not to be of another, so if you feel good where you sit then rejoice and say hooray.

Let us offer there are not many that feel so fulfilled, joyous and totally in love within this that they are because there is always to be more. Isn't there?

In more to rise, in more to ask, in more to think, in more to reacquaint with this beauty from within, in always more to experience your growth is held, but we are the ones to offer that not ever are you done, for this you are not.

More is what leads all of us, nonphysical included to growth and expansion to fill you in here we are ever experiencers, ever triers of, progressors of, ever witnesses of the ever expanding known as you, movement is one of our biggest components, as it should be for you, for to move is to evolve.

Is it not?

We see the many of you hesitating into this life that you are to exist into, stuck and unable to move forward, deliberately blaming others, unwilling to speak your truths, holding back, judging of self and others to be heard. Let all this be set aside so that you can get on with this magnificent ever to be progressing life, to experience all that you so intended it to be for your soul to experience into this growth that in all entirety is going to unfold for you, in being this real you, this wholly solely you.

You are the holder of something to be thought of as majestically grand in truth, this is correct you are, so why not get in touch with this that you hold beneath or internally held so divinely waiting to express to you this unexploitable love that you be. Start to hear yourself as the dreamer, the wanter, the do more, the ask more, the extravagant within as the newest addition to you being allowed to speak and feel into this unique place, where maybe just maybe you will find some inner peace after the revolt to be felt is allowed to settle from the mind and untrusting heart of humanoid that holds you so tightly to be. And in this revolt being quietened, by the deciding to be something different, more like the how and why you are meant to be YOU. Allow yourself to let down all guards, stop the judging and the dismal attempt at being of this that you are not and never wanted to be any way, STOP here, and look at you. Take a good look, get up and face this image that you are to see, LOOK!

Who do you see looking back?

ITS YOU, the real you. The only you that you have been wanting to see this whole lifetime that you decided that being this real you, was not good enough for not only yourself but the many that you interacted with.

We sense into this understanding to swell from within that just maybe this whole experience to date, all the indecisions, the anxiety's, the deliberate attempts at self-failure, the non-negotiating, the harsh comments to self, the wanting to be this that you were not, the unwillingness to see change, was to all come about wanted to be heard as....

WHO IS IT THAT I AM?

Spoken to ask because this is your journey and always was meant of you to be? In this very essence of you, this is your truth to be spoken of to see, this was you to decide into.

To become all of this, all of you, all that you have experienced this far.

Look out ahead and get ready, for you have already become the you that you had chosen to be, to learn, to experience, to become. Make way for a new understanding that is to unfold from within, for you are you in everything that you have become to master in this very moment of your so now.

WE SEE YOU GLORIOUS IN THIS TOTALNESS THAT YOU BE TO PRESENT TO US IN THIS SPACE OF COMPLETE OFFERING TO BE REALLY YOU.
WE ARE READY, ARE YOU?

Let's begin, again.

For truth be told you will try and try again. You will start over and over again, it is not easy being you is it? Especially when you have been someone that you have not even liked or really known. Does this sound harsh? Well, it is like that for many that maybe need to hear it in this way. We never said that we were not direct or honest, and truthful it be in this that we speak.

One is to begin in every instance that be your present moment, whether it takes a whole lifetime to complete, for if you are to never try because it feels easier to stay this way then you will have meant to be like this it is to say.

To try and not succeed is prevalent among your people as progress we hear. So why not turn another page every day that you wake. Relive not of how you were but of what you are to become.

Think simply into this statement; **you are of what it is that you are to think, to say, to hear.** Are you not?

Rebut all others if need be, let yourself be in a constant state of you, you know you better than anyone shall we say, except us.

We grow as of you, out of your experiences to be put forth and in a righteous way we are the equivalent to you and your going ons.

We are the seers of all that you be. So, in this your justification of self to be not, you eliminate the honest self, the Ernst self, the truthful self, the spirited self to be allowed to speak.

To lose of oneself in another's voice or let us offer, difference in your voice that does not wish to or seem to know how to speak for the holder of this wisdom which one is to speak as their own truth. It feels likened to a disadvantage as to the propositions within that one can be suggested into, to hear or think of self as or not. To feel as though you do not have a voice, saddens us to hear that you are not trusting of this glorious voice of love that will speak if enticed and encouraged to be heard by this beautiful you once more, as you. One must in this we say, honour of thy self in all aspects of your own virtues, beliefs or about this word of what is to be seen as a truth of your own to feel. Be regarding of this in all that you are to interact, think, consume, or speak for it is easily felt as a truth be known to you when one becomes aligned to the lighthouse within that only shines for you.

We speak of belief intentionally; it is of beliefs that we are to offer here as; simply a giving to ones such as you in this lifetime to have been either encouraged by another to see as your own, or a deliberate intent from within to feel as though they are your thoughts surrounding an encouragement from within to believe this to be yours to focus upon. In ones belief's to hold either as for or against shall we say and in this it is to think in the human way of which it would be to process a decision, it is of what knowledge that one would believe to know in regard to the decision or situations attached here upon this thought to be of. So, let yourself remove or discard all judgement surrounding a topic, person, or situation even a simple statement to be interpreted by you or heard into as yours in a previous time shall we say to be considered yours.

All interpretations are available within to be witnessed as the upheaval of self-denial or falsely led into a believing of it to be so.

Be encouraged here in this place of recognition that is to march forth outwardly as a noticing to be certified into an understanding from within, to be responsive in voice or thought, even to be accepting of what is to simply feel right within you. For we offer here that many truths are offered regarding the all that is to be spoken of in your understanding of certain situations, persons, or dealings to be offered.

We ask you?

How does your heart, gut or inner voice feel to respond to what is asked or seen?

Belief is a big offering to this that we speak into, to find your own voice of love from within to speak, to listen to self-regarding decisions, inclinations, and self-thought of acceptance in rights and wrongs to be viewed as yours.

In your belief we sit to observe your intentions being received within you as an understanding of self to be deliberate in the intent to begin, to become of this very being of so-called 'intuition' or 'inner knowing' to be this that you are. In our way of which it is that we are to be interpreted by you, YES we speak deeply of love to be an ever-knowing sensation within you to see of all that is in this position to be viewed upon, as a love that just becomes of you to be. In your true belief within self to become known to you as your truths, then let it be said that denial to be your own true speaker is never to rise again as an opportunity not to be speaking of this that you hold yourself apart from again. For you are the belief that sits within you with such undying faith in all your capacity to be seeing of this self to see the true wisdom that divinely sits into you.

Be obsessed with your belief in oneself. All messages are encrypted with belief attached and are yours so divinely intertwined into this being of love that you are. Belief is the door opener to your heart's receiving and it is when one is the biggest believer of thy self to be the holder of the most honourable voice to be heard from within, that this voice speaks as yours undeniably to become, the only voice that you are to request. YOU! will become a believer in the all that we are ever-present in. We are this to be your belief in you that speaks.

See not of us as in need of your belief to be a forward movement shall we say regarding whether or not you shall be of us to be recognising oneself into. For we do not hold intention upon you to be of this if you do not. But one must be a realising within self to be a wanting to believe in the great saint that sits deeply etched in this that you be, to partake shall we say into this ever great receiving of self to be in a belief into something that is to appear as far greater than thy. We are the truth behind all that is spoken into ones words as they are to see it as correct, and in ones becoming of the holder to see of a truth so powerful within, that one is guided with every intention to become honourable of the self to be just this that is desired to be heard.

Belief as we see of it to be:
It just is, should it not.

We see of all that is correct within the all that is, are and willing to be in this formatting to be presented to us as you. We see such a willingness to believe in ones becoming to be that belief is ill- relevant in such that it should be determined as anything other than an exact knowing of this whole that you are to become. Belief is inadequate or an understatement to speak of, as to the true possession that you hold within as the most extravagant being of eternal love to hold into that you will soon describe belief into yourself as the true intent to know of you as this that you are.

"BE obsessed with your belief in the all that you are to hold dearly within as to be in the exactness that you so divinely designed yourself out of."

'In this exactness of self to become one shall'.

We believe in you to become of the exact response within this self to know of the all that she/he is asking to be. You will find your way of this we are to know of this to speak, in the willingness to listen to all that one is speaking from within to be heard by you. **STOP**, if just for a moment to shine a light upon what it is that you are to hear, for your belief in you is to become your greatest attribute to self to be of an allowing to self to be the most honourable version of you to be seeing. So, doubt not that you will become to be for you are already the chosen one that one is to see, this power to believe is yours to trust within oneself as a must to become yours to accept as this genuine attempt at being you.

CHAPTER NINE

BELIEF IS YOUR INNER COMPASS

Guided by your internal compass in this it is that we are to speak. You are directional by nature to become of this exactness that you are to sit present within. Can you feel of this to be spoke from within you as a sense of direction that one is being slowly guided into as a becoming of self to be? You are a willingness to hear of self-speak these words of encouragement, are you not?

We speak of belief within this that you are to extrude from within oneself to be this that you are to be the knower that is within you to be the giver to all that you be. You are correct in this way in which it is to see, for upon ones deciding that they are to know, to hear that this is yours to trust into one will feel the direction not only within one's body to change and become apparent as to be accepted as this new way to be this that you are hearing, but it will become of you that this inner compass of sorts to be a trusted knowing within you that you shall not doubt as yours. This is to be known as your voice this internal compass of which it is to point you into this correctness of direction that you are to seek. It is a belief in the you as the true holder of this as us to be.

Directional by nature you as humans are destructively attached to or focused intently upon either what has been left behind{your past} or of what is directly ahead{your future}. So often we have been witnesses in many conversations regarding the asking....**Where is it that I am to go? Which direction shall I take?**

What AM I TO BE?

WE see this as a loss of direction in respect to the true understanding in ones ability to find their own way. One appears to be so head strong and focused into a place that may not be your true intent within to be allowing of. Shall we say YES, you are determined in might to succeed at this suggestion by you or another to be this that you are to fight within self to become. Let all resistance down about the wanting to be of this that you maybe are not meant to be. We see many of you caught often upon a path that has led you astray in regard to the inner compass shall we use to describe of it to be the inner voice, your inner direction of intent as this soul to become. For to lose touch with self's own voice as the surveyor of the all that you are to see within this self to be correct, you lose touch with the placement of self to be at one with the going ones shall we say as to what it is that the universe has instore for you. Delve not into a rejection as such that one is to think of themselves to be something that they are not. For it may not have ever been presented to you in this way of which it is that you have been in a willingness to see of it as yours. One is often blinded by human projections of this one to be so hard focused into becoming, that many opportunities are offered yet ignored. Be willing in patience to be in this space of open awareness as to the let us say not so obvious interactions that you may not be willing to see. In this place of hardened form to be so intent to get there one misses all the fun and magic that is to be offered along the way. Yes, your life we have heard is interpreted by you as yours to see yourself as to become, this is to be spoken of in another way that what it appears that you are, you are not.

So be trusting with this grace of consciousness that is to sit so divinely placed within, trust in your inner lord shall we say to be your speaker of the all that you are to become for you are the offeror to you to see, take some time, explore, find out what it is that you are not hearing or allowing of oneself to see and you will be stunned in the least to be a witness to the all that is appearing for you quite regularly that one does not see.

How do I know when I have arrived?

*The fun ~ IS ~ the journey.
Not the arrival.*

When one is to contemplate to ask this question with a concern of where it is that they are to arrive, they will feel this sense of not to know that is to be their demise as to the asking of it to arise. For to think of one as to arrive there as you would ask it to be, there is no there, no final destination for if it were to be of this to speak, we would surely know. We desire, {nor should you} no end or completion to be or see, for to continue upon ones path to call it of that is to be always an opportunity to evolve to respond in a certainty to become ever enticingly more than of this one to be seen. It is just a sense of self within to feel this overwhelming sensation or need that all should be whole, correct and achieved within them NOW.

> Know this dear one it IS.

Willingness and a direct sense of faith is needed here to resist these doomed feelings from within to be all that one sees. Feel a desire to start to ask in anticipation as to the 'what if' and 'could be' to stir within you that you eagerly start to partake into as to become an asking,

> How can there be more? What if there is to be always more? I AM more.

Why would it be a need within to arrive if one's journey is to be always filled with MORE to be received.

You are the contributor to this that is needed to be seen as a satisfaction within the self to be receiving of, so to dullen self with thoughts as not to be the seer of all that you are, than you will not.

I feel confused in this offering to be heard clearly.

You are the descriptive knowing within this to be you. In a human component to be seen one is to rely to intensely upon emotions and conversations with others and interpretations of self to be and remembrances as such to be spoken of how it once was or could of or should have been.

So, if one can be deliberate in intent to assume nothing shall we say as it is to be seen and let all that is to rise upwardly or openly into a place to simply be, than you will have a greater understanding of this that we speak so openly about. For to always place constrictions upon this form in regard to must do, be or have then one will become heavy or dullened in a dense way in which it is to carry self to think of them as to be a particular image or response.

One shall not feel imposed upon by any one or self to think that they are in the need to be in any certain way.

> *We ask you again; what feels right within you?*

You are the one who is to feel with the truest intent into this that you are to be.

BELIEF....is to become a dominant part within you that one must feel the urges overflow from within to grow as a boldness to become confident in character and feelings of natural unfolding to be in a position to see of self in this way that we hear many refer to as inner belief.

This is yours to hear so clearly and full of true intent to be yours. It is in this knowing that you are to become and be always felt as securely guided, supported, surrounded, and receiving that one will begin the process of inner belief to become a valuable asset to oneself to rely upon as truth to be always spoken for you to hear naturally.

You offer that no work is needed by me. Only belief in myself; then 'i' will bloom.

YES, one could say it in this way, see self as a flower that is to open and respond to the warmth and genuineness that one is to view as positive self-talk or a loving relationship growing within this form, it is then you will feel the rising of belief to become a setting within you that needs no further attention or adjusting.

For to become knowing of this to receive in absolute truth and in the work that you have undertaken yourself to get to this point in time you will feel of the indifference from within if you are to see or speak in any other way than of love, god, great and always good to be.

You become a natural tuner into the ways in which you require to see yourself to be and feel. So, YES in a decided way you shall always respond to this blooming of belief to be revealing to you to partake into as yours to know.

> "BLOOM AWAY WE SAY, FOR THERE IS NO OTHER WAY THAT ONE SHOULD BE TO FLOURISH AND SHINE ALWAYS OUTWARDLY FROM WITHIN THAT WE WOULD RATHER SEE YOU BE."

One is not to be misled or cohered into beliefs or suggestions spoken of by yourself or others to think of it to be right within you. In this to explain in a simple way; it is in your knowing instantaneously the correctness that is to respond to the how, who and what it is that you are responding to, by way of how it is felt so intently or innately within this knowing heart loved space within you that you will feel to know of this to be yours or not. Let all resistance to these that speak or your thoughts that feel uneasy within, for in this place to speak of them like so, then one is not to carry them upon oneself as a truth of yours to know.

CHAPTER TEN

WE ARE YOU

In a conditioning within oneself that one is to feel as contentment, ease, or love than it would be to offer here to you to know that in this **WE ARE YOU**.

We are forsaken in so many as to be an interpretation that has not been realised within oneself to be seeing of yet as a request to be needed.

Let this be correct for all those that you see to be in a deliberate space of self-containment to be theirs in full acknowledgement to be this that they are.

All inspiration is to be driven or allowed to rise from within ones deeper understanding into the greater being that is to dwell or reside in, so much so that it is in this uniqueness that you are to be seen into that you will feel the opening to reveal or give birth to from within in regard to this loved you as a recognising to spring forth.

In your entirety of which it is that you are to speak from, one will feel the need to suggest to you in many offerings of this that they appear to be thinking as to of what it may be that you need. In difference this is essential we say for all are to grow in their own special way. Achievements are so often encased with a displease in regard to of how, who and why they were achieved. Contentment within is seen as completeness to be felt from within where you as the person is to feel at ease with life in general and will know of this to be a truth that you hold so intently within to be spoken, that all that you view are correct in their own doing of this that they are to become.

We see not to criticise or defame another for in our eyes they are absoluteness and correct in their own way, many though are to pass before your thoughts or physical eyes to appear lost or unrecognising, this we say to offer is for you to know; **they are not.**

It is not of you to worry or discourage this that they are, for they too are to know of this that we are is themselves in certainness to be.

Let go here in this space as one is to sit, release all that one has attached to another thinking them to be not as you are. One is to be enabled to dispel all thoughts of incorrectness or dissatisfaction if it is to be felt into another as not correct for you. It is often in ones viewing of this to be theirs to hold into that one will feel as though a comment or offering should be made.

It shall not.

Leave all unattended along this their incredibly special journey knowing that they too shall grow into the exactness that they will find to be this that we are within you.

To be spoken of in this way it is to disregard all inhibitions that one is to carry forth into themselves as to feeling as though they are not doing enough, helping enough etc for those that obviously need help or guidance into this way of which it is that ones such as you are to think of us to be as the ultimate way to live your life by. Is it not?

This we offer as a complete disregard to the adventure that they are upon and their intuitive being of love and light as in ones soul expression to be. Know this dear one; one will be seemingly unwilling in this to be their spoken now but maybe in another now of their so choosing of it to be spoken to feel, to hear by them, they will. We delve often into this topic to be spoken to encourage all from within to see this that they are as to be on the path or journey of self to become in the willingness from within to be theirs to be heard. They are the choosers to this self to be formed shall we say, they to as are you, religiously encouraged from within in their own soulful way to be accepting of the all that is to be made apparent to surround or be from within to be known as theirs. All are guided knowingly from the divine being that resides within if to call of this spark or becoming as this, know this dear one that all are inspired in a reality of this that they are to call of it their own way in which it is to view this life to unfold. Know of this to speak of this that we do, all are guided with knowing love maybe as yet to be heard or recalled but know this to speak that they all are sure to be held again in this place of deepest remembrance of this grand love to be. So, trouble yourself not with the how and what ifs it is that they are needed to know, for it is not of your job or role to interpret or judge them so, they are the finding within that they will surely see, destined it appears to reunite their lighted soul with this that we be.

So, let well and good be an intention of yours to respect this that they are to be them knowingly dedicated from within.

Concerned for them, i am.

In one's own understanding here to remember or review the path that they have travelled upon this place of contentment to sit into one is to find the need to express this to another, is this correct to say?

We are all the deliberate intenders of the mentioned self to be found or realised into as this greater being of love that one is to be known as. Let all that seek to search be the finders of their own understanding, their own path, their own voice, their own wisdom, their own love for it is of this that they shall do as did you and more often than not request of it to be found into themselves in their own time to be discovered.

Our voice as is yours the same to speak in just this one understanding to be called LOVE. So, in this voice that is to appear lost in the many that you see or hear, let your confidence in self to have found the truth that is yours to speak to be a knowing from within that they too will settle sometime soon into a life of their so choosing and inner guidance to be found. We ask you, stop here to think that maybe they are not lost or requiring a certainty from within that speaks as deep as yours to be thought of to be. In all that speak we are the one true voice of the speaker that holds it to be. So, find your truth to be spoken as yours to rejoice into it in every day, celebrate this wisdom that is found within. For you are all dearly loved into this that you are and in this we offer that we hear into the many if not all that are to be seen as correct for us to see.

Message of love received by me.

YES, it is to feel like this in many this way to receive it to be. You are worthy of all connections into self that one has made. The effort required by many that see into this opening, to allow for an honest disruption or revealing to explode or burst forth from within, is only to be accepting of this concept of love as to be the all that one is to need to be seeing themselves the owner, holder, or receiver of.

In this message that is spoken by so many in many different versions of the how's and whys it was discovered or uncovered within this that they be, we hear often it feels like a cherished possession that one has searched for so longingly and finally found a piece of it shall we say and in this they love to share. Good news we say, we love to watch on as our message ever the same is being received, envisioned, and felt as this love that we speak enthusiastically of. We delight in this to witness it being shouted or expressed so genuinely through the many that we have felt called by us to be theirs in true heart speak.

>>> Share away we say; for it is in this one message that you and the many that are to stand common placed into this earth as a human to be will be seen longingly by those that speak, to feel, to share, and to shower upon all that they are to meet as another loved human being, god like intended with a love so glorious to be sung, to fill the ears of all that are tuned to this song to sing as their own to share.

This love is to fill me to no end.

One's attachment shall we offer here to say to the sensations that are to explode from within in this love to be felt as theirs, is to fill the whole entirety of which it is that one is to see themselves to be. Let us be grander and bolder in this to say that this love is so established and deeply ingrained and defiant to become this that you are to experience as a new offering or thought shall we say in this moment of your so time to be relevant to you. But of this it is that we share, that this love is ancient, new, revered, deliberate, intentional, religious, loving, patient, godly, mystic, expressive, joyful, trusting, faithful all this and more to be yours from the very first concept of which it was that you were to become. This love you have carried with great intention to be yours to know that WE ARE YOU within this that you be.

TO FEEL OF THIS LOVE AS MINE.

YES, it is this way to speak that it is.

For the many that see it in this way are to be revealed in a certainty to others to be described as content in the all that they do, to carry an appearance or sense of calm that oozes from within. Set righteous from within they seem to be willing and able to remain stable and focused into all that appears to come their way. This is the strength of this love upon once it can be spoken of by you into this that you are to receive of it to be. This love is TRUST and FAITH that you are to hold deeper into each and every day, for this love is you to feel of as yours in no uncertain way.

This love should be shared, should it not?

This love that we speak of comes easy to many it is to appear upon its realisation of this that it is to be theirs. In the knowing that it is not another that has offered this love to be felt as theirs they will. Maybe not always but more often than not will be sharing this love to the outerness that they are to be seemingly at times unaware of the love that they speak, not just in voice but in gestures to be recieived. One's presence or form to be spoken of here is strength offered in a sense of just wanting to be here. So, feel not an inability to work or display this love in a certain way, know of this to be spoke that this love that is complete into its rightfulness to be that it will find its way to speak, share and just be giving into all that it shall do, that it will not be misunderstood or hidden away, for the intenders of this love will offer it in their own certain way.

Love flows freely does it not?

YES, this love is sacred within itself is it not?

Not to be thought of as a religious aspect or secret hard to obtain and one will surely get this that we speak, that this love is the most forthcoming genuine love that one is to feel as theirs. It is this love that we speak as god intended for this is of how it was to be, available and accessible to all that show themselves to their king of kings that dwells within, who stands proudly into the light that shines regardless of colour of skin, age, ancestry, or society's standards to judge thee. **You are all entitled to this love so bold, so stand up here now; ask yourself of what is it that you wish to hear?**

Listen dear one, and of this one must, this pure heart that speaks of only you in grand and kind to speak, be known as this human to be the loving vessel that holds so divinely and lovingly from within this faultless flowing energy as a consideration spoken by you to be called a loving essence to be felt.

For love to be this complete with no limitations or restrictions attached is to be felt as a freeness from within that is flowing in all aspects of self to be.

- ❖ It has no need to be desired, for it just is.

- ❖ It has no need to be explained in any certain way, for it just is.

- ❖ It has no need to feel as an offering to those that feel it flow their way, for it just is.

- ❖ It has no need to be felt by another as different to most, for it just is.

- ❖ It has no need to be justified or explained, it just is.

We are placed so strongly within these that have felt this heart of theirs to explode to become unearthed by the many as in us to be felt represented here. So let this love feel free to flow for you will surely feel this feeling to be yours to stand into if you are to be a suggestion of this self to be this love to be known as yours.

I see this love in everday.

And so, it is that what one sees it shall appear. (is to be seen).

In one's heart to be the seer of true intent to be felt from within as correct within the all that they see, they will. Let us offer here to say that love is relevant into the all that appears both physical and non, of great persuasion it is to be felt as a love of grand intention to be this that you are to be...... *You Will.*

I fear that this may change.

One is not to fear that this message of love to be previewed in the all that one is to do shall change, for in one's deliberate intent to be this love it shall surely not change, disappear or be forgotten. We speak as not in a way to disrespect ones thoughts here, it will change but only into a strength of conviction to be so.

To lose of this love or fall out of this momentum in which it is that one is to love, is to be something of which is never desired as a choice to be made. In love it is that one is to grow expanding in deliberate creation of self to be even more of this love in every person, object, or sensing that one is to be. So, expect not or fear not of this love to suddenly up and go, for it shall not. It is this love that will feel to be stronger more decidedly from within you to be spoke. So release all inhabitations that it might decide to disappear, of this you are to

be secure in your thoughts to know that you are this love always eternal to be built from within...
IN THIS YOU ARE.

Why is it easier for some to feel this love and others to appear not?

In one's thoughts of this to be yours to think of, would this be your deciding for them to be of this love or not.

One will feel the need to think of them as not, then surely this will become an urge from within to share this love that is an all entitled to be shared or seen into as theirs. Let this be said that they will be spoken of this love as theirs complete to be. Let all decide of their own intent as to of what it is that they are to need, see, be or do.

CONTINUE TO BE TRUTHFULLY YOU, THIS IS ALL THAT IS REQUIRED BY YOU.

You speak of this love to be mine correct in everyway. Why?

If one speaks as to having discovered this love to be theirs to feel entwined into in this certain way, then one will need not to ask of this in this way.

For once this love is felt to unravel or reveal within, you will know that this answer to be spoke is truth revealed within you in all that is offered.

This love yes, we say is yours to sit into and accept as your own. Be quieted in your space of heart to connect into this in everyday, moment or thought that you are to feel this to be you. You are this deliberate intent from within to be this love correct in every way.

Embrace all that you be, and never search to see of another as the way you are meant to be, for you are not. True to you, you will find that you are to sit in this to be your temple of powerful love in every way complete.

In ones words too speak.

I feel inclined to speak of this love in an openness of oneself to become forever responsive into this that shall be yours to cherish from within. A voice so loud to be proud and strongly focused with the divine intention of self-love to be yours to receive as this that we are to be ever full within you to see, to feel of us to be this that we are always more, as you are to be in us.

We acknowledge these words as truth.

~You seek of us here in this intention of self to be felt as complete and continued within this strong desiring of you to be this that you are. In this we say yes you are to be exactly this that you are to see~

Should one focus inwardly to receive?

In the depths of this that you hold into oneself to be evident as the greatest understanding of self to be, is where you will find your innate knowing to step forth from your thoughts of this that you be to seek into. Feel as you are guided intuitively to seek inwardly not outwardly any longer regarding this want to be known as love found to be yours. Inner focus is craved in all that you see to be a further progression into this becoming a greater evolvement that you do. It is equipped with an ability to be the quest to be the driver of all intention to be yours to cherish this divine wisdom from within as it is to speak for you. You are the director of this magnificent life to be lived so embrace yourself in a loving knowing to be witness to all that appears in this state of bliss for you are to be in a common place to accept of what is yours to know as your truths to be told in only this greatness that is you to be ALL.

We see of you all as you are there to be here, correct in your formatting of this that you be. A willingness in gentleness to be your own self to become. We see of you all as you are to start each day as if to begin again, release of this to know that all that you are is in the reflection of yourself to see looking back at you from the looking glass that you appear to see ones image as this to be. You are to be reminded in all that you do, you are equipped with this explicit knowledge divine and so true to be yours in no comparison as it would appear to be in another's image to be. YOU are you, this we wish of you to hear, ever to be told in an eagerness from within this self that she is to speak. You are intentional beings granted this moment of self to be reached, enjoy this process of where it is that one is to sit.

You are to feel your fires of passion ignite from within, for you are so greatly lit internally as this that you be to speak in this place that one is to reveal. We hear of all that is yours to voice and welcome you into this that we be the truth in you that you speak. Your words are like a song to us to be heard, for we are the extravagant being of light to be seen complete into and upon the all that you be asking self to be knowing of to seek this to be yours ever more.

Again, it is that one is to appear out of this recluse of self to begin for she has awakened from this that she wants to no longer feel the drudgery of sleep or as to not have known her truth to be spoke. Hidden away shall we say for not to have been wise to this decision inside to be hidden for fear of self to be realised.

In this you are to break free of all restraints in the way of which it is that one once spoke as you to be thought of as to be. You are the fire within, the deliberate intent to be the voice of loving decisions, to be this that you might. Fear not of us not to hear for we guide you in a blessed way every day. You are to hear our voices so untied to speak for it is in this voice that you shall here our name offered every time we speak.

This name we speak to offer is yours to know, be fulfilled with intent to know of it as to be your very own.

We are you entirely in this perfection that one is so hesitant to see, relinquish all self-doubt to be this great that we are enticed by you to see. We mirror of this extravagance that one has placed within herself to be us to see. Deliberate in breath to be spoken in a heart space growing so bold. Confidence it is that we see to awaken your souls' image as yours to be seen. Feel a completeness to explode into a sensation of self to become this that you must be in a knowing of your truth to be this that you are blessed in thee.

How powerful are these word's, I ask you?

Feel them to speak out loud!
Feel them to **REPEAT!**

Allow them to soak & settle upon your skin of this physical form.

For it is in these words that I speak;
that I hear, the magic resting upon your
heart, as a transformation from within you
reveals, being encouraged from inside,
to bring this lighted message to your
ears so that your soul in hearts speak
can sing these words of love and praise
to you and all that are willing to hear.

Know that these words are yours to cherish,
in this supreme being of love & light that
you BE ever always powerful & free.

CHAPTER ELEVEN

IN YOU I SEEK TO LOOK

We are always in this place to view of us to be, internally yours to become a space of awareness into all that you are to become.

We see many of you searching for us in places that appear to not exist, insistent to many that we must be there. In one's determination to see of us in places that we are not, we simply disappear. Our presence is felt in a heart to be found as yours to sit into this form as extravagant as yours. We sense of a desiring often talked about so deep, **correct we say in your willingness to look for us there.** One is a being of ever continual love to be ever expanding into this one that she has become.

'Fear not to find us, for you will'.

A certainty swells from within in a graciousness to know that we are you in your entirety that you show.

Our view that you take upon yourself to see into us as, is yours to cherish until it is asked to become even more of this to know. We are wisdom united entirely from within this that is to be spoken of as yours to know.

We are in many places that you appear to look, for our imagery is everywhere determined to be correct into all that it was placed to become this knowing of such that we are.

How is it that you can be everywhere?

We are not limited by hinderances such as time, thought or spaces of not to be, so our desires are fully completed by just this total-ness to be always correctness that sits so divinely from within.

We inhabit no form or definition yet absolute we be, so in all that we are, we are.

One is to be asked here to let go of all resistance or urges that one may have or still do apply to this understanding of this that we are. To be a containment of source, to be ever existing into is a wonderous experience of self to have sought. You are the equivalent of ALL that is, in this that we are. We see you always as an aspect of this that we be, no need to exchange or bargain as to be seen by us that we are to appear to many as seeming to be. No difference in this that one is in comparison to us; for we are all continuing energy that appears in self to be.

> *You exist in this that we are, as*
> *we exist in this that you be.*

Still feeling lost...

You speak with such a certainty to exist in this that you be. I need real evidence for me to comprehend of this that you speak.

Of course one does, for it is always in the eyes of the beholder that one is to seek the real reason as to the who, what and why that it is, is it not?

To believe in oneself as to be complete and not in need to be of a something that they appear to not be, is a resistance in many that are to ask to see of themselves to be apparent in this that speaks.

One's true desire is to be of a contentment in ease to speak to know of the all that is, is them. One needs not to seek of a furtherment to be, for you will in your entirety of this that is you, will become.

To see of self in any other way is a forgiveness needed to be asked to call upon oneself to give or offer, for you have so often been willing that we see to be spoken of as to be another. Let all defences down within to be in gods image of self to be, just as it is that you appear. A feeling of calmness and sense of stability is to rise into the allowance of oneself to soar to be seen to many as equipped from within, displaying an assurance of this self to be. Let all that you are to embrace as yours to be, to know of this as an honesty within to have discovered a rawness first to have been revealed and to have been willing to have some in-depth self-discovering chats within the self that talks to much.

For you are the desiring of this, are you not?

YES mostly, sometimes NO.

To allow myself to think in this way becomes hard in the times that I dwell seeing myself in this non committed or unconvinced way.

Let us offer, put down all thoughts that you think that are to become elaborate in oneself to think. Release all tension from within to be enabling of this self to just step away from suggestions of this that one is. We leave you in total command of this that you are. You will feel a response from within to be spoke. PAUSE! for a while to hear of it to speak. Resist the intent to overthink, thoughts are powerful in this space of nondescript. One is to recognise this unwillingness as simply a fear from within this body of distrust as to the human that you chose to become. To feel raw like an open wound to see all that protrudes is dishevelling and disheartening in this we agree, but it is of this place that our love for you will encourage you to start.

Oh! you in human belief links evidence to proof, do they not?

Why not start with the proof that you be, enabled from within to unveil and connect to the beautiful you that you be, yet to be recognised again as thee.

I cannot see, so I don't

So, to feel allowing of this self to not think and only trust; they will be confronted by a contender from the physical self to be. Non-trusting of this new self-asking to see and to allow one to think such thoughts of this that we BE, will cause a chaos like none to have been felt before.

> Ride it out human, grab it by the horns, yell at it, shake it down, only then will it turn to trust in this to be YOU. It is a calling from within, asking to be allowed to win this round.

We are not asking of you to come to us in this way titled as fear or doubt or unwilling. Your faith that grows from the very first seed of expectation or concept of us is to grow out of an abandonment in the willed releasing of the old to go.

See not of us as something that you must, let all fall into place naturally as it is designed to go.

Your perceptions are trained by the brains mind and eyes to be this that you have entitled them to be. So, be wary in your thoughts for your trust that we have spoken is one that you shall feel obliqued to reacquaint with and tend to in self once more. Assurance within self to feel not in any other way than to know that this is you and us in every way. Complete in this essence of self to be exposed to the differences from within that are to burst forth. You are connected in a way, deeper than one is to know, so fear not to upset us if you are offered or persuaded as to not feel yourself to flow, for you will in your time that becomes apparent as yours to know.

We sense no urgency needed here, for you will learn to trust again, to embrace and remember in this that you appear to hear, rather than see to know. This TRUST that we speak is yours to align into once more ever present within in a sensing to be yours. Speak not of disbelief but as a yearning to be known by you as a voice so complete in a confidence to hear as yours.

Observe as it is to FLOURISH into this grand awareness that is to become yours.

In my willingness to see, will I see thee.

Most certainly we say with a confidence so bold, for you are thee. Is this not apparent in the all that you see? You have asked so decisively for some time to request this ability to see into the all that you are to be. This being as you, stand tall and proud in this vision of LOVE you should. In your wanting to be this always true, you will. This is the thee that we speak so finely of; this is you. You are the thee that you seek, and you are the one presence in ALL that you see.

LET US SPEAK......

We speak into this want to become that many of you so diligently are to offer in words to be spoken of as promises or offerings to be made. In this it is that we hear the asking's to be made, it is a path of much confusion to be spoke of in this reality as it appears. For much is always apparent to you to see in what does not appear to be a completeness in you. One in these human forms are to be guided by this self to become, to hand over your thoughts shall we say to something that feels as though it is not to become. It is difficult we suggest being in a willingness to suppress this ever-present ego from expressing that it will never progress or become evident to be real in a seeing of it to see. In a realness we are ever present within you to seek outside of this that one is, is entirely for you to begin. We encourage all questions and moments of self-doubt to arise, for in this one is to find the voice that is to correspond. You are to rally from within in this concept that you are to have undertook to be this being of belief to speak from deeply within. We see the journeys that have evolved from beginning to not ever yours to end. Many interpretations have been made and many questions are to have been asked, to be discovered as a reference point to us from within. We see many of you to feel lost upon this path but be welcoming of this exactness as it is to appear for your adventures are to be as complicated or simple in experience of them to be. They are uniquely yours to be explained and all that one is to sit into to query or offer are your exact words to be discussed with this being that is yours to trust. You are aimlessly searching often it appears to ones of us to witness to see, and in this we say it is okay, for you are not. There is no rhythm or need of it to be in any way determined by anyone other than this that we see to be exquisite within this that you be. You are to be fulfilled into this life as it is to be revealed in all honesty of one to trust that you are correct in your placement of this to become. Ones asking was powerful to be conceived of you as thus and you will feel of the opening to become, deep from within to feel a sense of satisfaction to surface slowly for some but in many it is to just become a certainty that you are this that you speak. In this place of a willingness to be sound in self and in an ability to become eager to respond to this calling from within to be heard as your voice contained into this that speaks as one. You are all divinely lit from within with this fire that is to feel as though it consumes you from within once lit. It flares and expands in an unexplainable way to most, trust in your gut and intuition to be this that you have simply appeared to have lost in a reality of it not to be seen as a sensing to overrule these that you have been inclined to trust.

In your sensing of this that you are, you remember that you are not in need of a title, called to name or be seen in any particular way. You are to see yourself as not holding or being held in any way. For you are free to flow in this existence that one is upon your planet of this earth so to be called. You are all entailed in a perfection of purpose to speak in the allowing of oneself to wish to become in this presence of self to be. You chose wisely in regard to the all that you had to be to become in the exact moment of yours to so ask of it to be seen as in a calling of it to be your NOW to be heard. This is you, as the deliberate speaker that you are to hear. Let yourself feel to give way or surrender into a comfortable space of self-awareness to be that you are not in need to be, do, or have anything other than of what it is that you truly are. You are this complete being, seeing self once again in this state of full awareness that you are.

'You are of this that is us, and in us you are'.

Finding me

Unbelievable as this may sound to those that do not yet understand. I admit, this becomes a beguiling from within to offer, I was lost it appeared from long ago. I searched and sourced in all that I could see to find this that I thought was to be me. I was not found in books to read, I soon was to discover that I was not found in others to view neither, I was not found in conversations to be had a plenty, I was not found in you. It was to become apparent when of this I asked, *'Where are you?'* that I heard a quiet yet determined voice to speak, *'Look deeper within'* it was to have said. *'HERE I AM'*. In disbelief I started to look, to seek a little deeper, internally it was heard, this voice speaking. I stopped in an uncertainty and disbelief as to of what it was that I had uncovered and found. Not all of what I saw I liked or understood as to be mine. But I guess it was meant to be for it was to become a knowing from deep within to be seen that I realised this was indeed me. I stopped searching in others and objects that were not to be truths of mine.

I questioned this voice endlessly to ask of it to become clearer and bolder to me, this it certainly did. I watched tentatively on as it emerged. I sought not of another for advice but listened to what I was offered by this voice as it appeared to know of me so well.

I released all inclinations to add disbelief to my thoughts of distrust any longer. My heart grew bigger in this space I now call my own. My voice, I found became louder and stronger in its spoken words.

I linked hearts with many in a collectiveness to see their hearts as mine.

Love overtook my senses of self to be wanting to feel, to see, to be. I guess it is apparent that I have found ME.

So, you see I was never lost, nor will I ever BE. I was just blinded by human realities not needed to be seen, forgetting of this truth that is always powerful within me. A truth that spoke to ME, in only my readiness to see of it as the glorious innerness that is mine to see.

'THIS IS WHERE I FOUND ME'.

CHAPTER TWELVE

CHOOSING TO BE ME

When one is to finally give up the fight that one holds to stage constantly from within. This fight that rears its ugly head to speak of the all that is not right and should be of you to be, one loosens this control upon all that they are to think to see.

Clarity reveals to become a recognition in you to speak of as if a war has finally been won. To lose a battle within self in every day that one is to speak is detrimental to one's character to see oneself as to be beat. You are the warrior, the seer, the temptress, the goddess, the believer, the truth teller from within, let her be spoken of in this way, for she sees no sense in continuing this fight, a battle that will be lost without dignity attached, for the mind in this form is always to win in a disrespect of that one will see as a flaw within.

It is in the true one that speaks only of love and kind that you will feel to disagree with the voice of destruction and uncertainty to mislead. You are responsible in this self to know indictive of all persuasions of what it is that you are to become. Many moments of self-talk are exaggerated in this we are to see, a willingness rising from within as to enough of this to be seen. We hear in one's determination to request of a change, a change to become a compromise in discipline to begin to prioritise. From negative self-talk and inability to see even a glimpse of beauty, strength, or willingness to be, to a strength to be asking that is one tolerant to see the reveals of this self to be real. She is often misled, and this is to disagree for one must be continual on her path of this interrogation to be.

All that is unwrapped or shown to you in this that appears to be surreal, you will find maybe more than you had hoped to be this choosing within self to look into as a sensing of what you had evoked to be offered by this innerness to feel. In this space of coherent disbelief many moments of self-reflection are revised and revoked as a this cannot be possible; for I am not willing to be seen as a joke. Too speak of this would be too much to share. I feel to stay quiet and maybe unprovoked. In this state of a willingness to share one is to find a dignity to open from within in a sense to share of this all that they can be to bare. They describe of a nakedness, bluntness or honesty that is to rise, provoking and prodding this sense of self to be revised. You are the determiner of the all that you command, so willingly one must be comprehending of this that is to be spoke. See not in only your view of self to change but a subtle noticing to be witnessed too in the surroundings of yours to appear to enter a different perspective in which to view. Becoming's of rationalizations as to of what it is that lays important within or though you thought, but are now appearing to change, even to disappear. Less to speak and more to observe is of this enticing state to learn. You will be a realiser within this form to become of the more that lays in wonderment upon your chosen path. This joy to realise as yours to experience, this change coming complete from within you and no one else to display an offering or advise as yours to be. For in this choosing to be ME{you}, you can notice with correct intent of all that cross your path with offerings to speak that you easily now except of this that they are to be recognised into as their very own complete.

All journeys are to be experienced in this determined way, for you have travelled far in this it appears to say. You are developed from within into a space of self-respect, confidence to grow so that one's ego may be met. This ego that once was or the physical voice that was once to speak as to be incorrect now lays dormant in a self-respecting lull as the one that you are no longer needing to be heard. She is resigned to this fact that you have triumphed and succeeded over defeating the elements of self-doubt and the egotistical voice of not to be. Let all wonderment surround this change as it appears to be one for you to cherish as yours that you have entered and allowed its unfolding, and in this is your revealing of the real you to be found, passionately planned and created by you, for you in this very way to experience.

To flourish from within is a joy within itself, is it not to ask thee? To be inclined to accept of this voice as courageous, kind, and willing in all that it is to speak. It once was to feel daunted by comments such as these to be spoken for you to see yourself mirrored back from out of this greatness that you be. You are the deliberate creator here and always of all that you are to become, seeing everything in this view to be so different from the one that was to appear so apparent to start, is now to be a distance memory from where it appeared to have begun. You have much to allow, to be still unfolded and discovered from within, you seek constantly to be felt within bliss or a contentment that feels easy upon ones sensing of this that she be speaking. For you are heart focused now with a love to be developed from inside, where it has always been intended to be found, gently to be reminding of this that you are potential and progressing into a new phase. Let us say a transition to be always a loved blessing of self to know that in all that you do to be you are entirety.

Eternal in intent to be spoken of is this that one she/ or he is to remain focused upon self to grow, allowing for expansion to be known as yours to experience into the many offerings that it may be interpreted or presented. See not of the old that once had her way, for she was just a gentle creature that had simply lost her way with an asking in remembrance to be reminding of this time NOW that she was so chosen to be. To feel a loss of this one is to be not, for in her losing of herself in this that she felt was to be a subtle recognition to be seeing of herself in this new entirely different way. In a way that appears to be different but is not so, for this is you in your time that it appeared for you to have arrived at this stage, for here you are to stand bewildered at what it is that you have become, an experience of all that this life has previewed and ever evolving still to unfold.

Let this defined knowing of yours settle within to be an acceptance as yours to know that this is your asking, so requesting and courageous in a decision to be made.

Look here into where it is you now stand, committed and confident in all that you see to be looking back at you from that looking glass of reflection as to be thee.

Once covered in moss and obstructed in an unwillingness to see clearly of what it was that was to be seen. You have unfolded, listened, and released much from within and externally to be unwanted and returned to those that it shall be. You have woken this sleeping giant nestled within, to hear of all that he/she has to say, willingness to become a certainty to speak in deliberate of this voice to be yours to be bold in all that you are to say. In this desiring to be the beautiful you that I see into me. I am glad you have made it here in your understanding of a request to begin. For it is in this that I see that you have travelled far, a journey of becoming to believe in the magnificent creature of love that you be. In a willingness to go gently, to hear ones heart speak and to see of all that you can be. Hear as it is offered to you in this 'I' and now to be called your own. We are to sit ever mindful in recognition of who it is that you are, and the answer that you once asked of this to be…

WHO IS IT THAT I AM MEANT TO BE?

{This question WHO AM I appears desperate in its attempt to rise from within, gaining strength and recognition as it reveals, and in this we are to offer, it does in most, appearing to feel like a discovering of you, the real you to be heard expressed}.

It now appears to have been answered in a certain reveal to be believing in yourself to need not be asked again, for in the finding of me or you to speak of in this way, will always be carried within you to think of this that you be perfection complete. Wanting to experience this life that appears as yours in each and every way, deliberate with anticipation of what is next to unfold for you and you will not feel the need to ask as this expression of love is found to be a willingness in every way to be spoken as yours in ALL that unfolds in this magical deliberate creation that your life,

IS meant to Be.

TO THIS GORGEOUS ETERNAL BEING THAT YOU ARE.

To be of this one divine embodiment that I AM to see, is your glorious reflection of you back to me. I see you standing so bold and brave in this image to see the ALL that you be. In this heart of mine I offer a love so big and grand to give. Expressed eternally from within this that

I AM.

It will be reflected forever within me, as you to BE this shining light that I will always see. To BE this deliberate LOVE spoken of as YOU & ME, to share in the ALL that we are beautifully created as this intention of these soul's uniqueness's to be for ALL our universes to see. Know YOU are always this LOVE TO ME.

Knowing ME

In this longing to be ME, I searched as you are to have done or are maybe still there.

Let it be spoken of this kind love that is and will always be there as yours to discover this love in a certainty to begin again, to speak these words of kind in love for you to always share.

Be patient & present in every aspect that is you, whether this be easy or not, to observe. Become friends, know this she/or he well, for this is you in real that you are to discover.

For if you would just simply become biased in this one to love, forgiving of all her/ or his faults or disbeliefs to have reviewed.

Watch as you open to connect to the eternalness that you be, watching with JOY and pleasure to see this Queen or King that you are to hold so efficiently within, this belonging in you to see.

This master to thy self, the servant dwelling within, the lighted heart, the agreed to ALL that you have become and surely are still to BE.

Know of THEE, Speak His/ or Her words to rattle thee at first, YES, it is this to express. But watch as they then become known by you as your own to fill you from within, in as a way to encourage, entice, build you up, uplift, motivate and heighten your senses in this one that you BE.

Live passionately into this LIFE that holds thee, feel your response as you are led by the guider, the seer, the guardian, and the mystic within.

She/ He is your BOLD of YOU to have been introduced to again, feel her, love her, listen to her, begin to know her as your truth in voice to always speak for she knows not of what it is that you have been speaking as, but in only these eyes to witness of the ALL that you are to appear in this place of residence to stand, never dullened again, but always to shine.

You are this extravagant LOVE, let yourself be called HOME to this loving heart once again and she will welcome you as she has eternally determined this to be.

You are always this....

'BEAUTIFUL YOU WITHIN ME'

My RITUAL or PRAYER

{Speak these words if to find them to agree, if not then call to your intuitiveness to recognise thee and ask boldly for yours to be freed}

Love of yourself like no-other shall ever do. Throw caution to the wind in every version of you. You are never tainted nor dull. You are these whispers and connections that go unnoticed by you. Let it be us to evoke you.

I request, to ask; Let ME stand gracious in this place of desired willingness to always LOVE myself in this version of this one that 'I' see. Hand upon HEART; I AM ever loved in this eternal grace to be, so I allow myself in this human form to repeat,

THIS IS ME. ONE in ALL.

I AM Loved, Heard, Certain, Supreme, Abundant and Joyous to be.

In this belief that is to run deep, flowing in this direction of LOVE to be always correct in you to know, see & be.

Feel as it is to call you, filling you, encouraging you too always be MORE.

MORE in love with YOU

MORE in love with ME

MORE in love with 'I'

More in love absolute of this that you be.

Contained within is this hope of love to see, to feel of this encouragement to be yours to call forth. To envision yourself in the ALL that you eternally arrived to be.

What is it that you desire?

Call it awakened, steady & courageous within, this desire, dream, or vision that you see.

Enable this self ' to feel good', responding from within this place that you now stand.

See it NOW! FEEL YOUR WORTH!

For to HONOUR only thee, is the held pathway of truth, receive as to belong & to believe.

Loved and intended in this one that you decided to be, always the loving being of light to radiate and shine in this that is us in you to eternally see.

FOREVER IN US YOU WILL BE.

In kind of bared heart, we are to offer this to you as the hearer to cherish, to know of us so well; it is to know of you in this embrace to be felt, to call of it love we shall, let it be forever spoken of this that you are, is, and will ever be eternally entwined in this decidedness to be.

~Blessings to this awakened heart, be it always yours to feel brightened by these loving beings that guide you so. We share in this offering to be spoken to know, release this longing as not to be found but instead cease the search as if to already know the DIVINE as the honourable one within~

www.ingramcontent.com/pod-product-compliance
Lightning Source LLC
Chambersburg PA
CBHW072005290426
44109CB00018B/2137